W9-BMZ-476

Sudbury, Massachusetts: 1890-1989

100 Years in the Life of a Town

Curtis F. Garfield

Courtesy of
Sudbury Historical Society, Inc.
P.O. Box 233
Sudbury, Massachusetts 01776

PORCUPINE ENTERPRISES
106 Woodside Road
Sudbury, Massachusettes 01776

Manufactured in the United States of America

First Edition

The author gratefully acknowledges the generous support of the
Sudbury Foundation, The Sudbury Historical Society, the Sudbury
Board of Selectmen and the Wayside Inn.

Printed By
Berryville Graphics, Berryville, VA

ISBN No. 0-9621976-3-7

Dedication

To Herb and Esther Atkinson
Whose generosity through their Sudbury Foundation
has touched the lives of all who live here.

Table of Contents

The Fifties: Houses and Schools, and Taxes, Oh My!

The Sixties: Conflicts Within and Without

The Seventies: Hornets Under Sudbury's Coat Tails

The Eighties: Rags and Riches and Two and One Half

Acknowledgements

Finding the information to explain 100 years of the history of Sudbury is a daunting task, and one that could not have been accomplished without the aid of a great many individuals and groups who have gone far beyond the call of duty to be helpful.

Special thanks go to Town Clerk Kathy Middleton and her staff who made available pertinent records from the Town Vault as well as the use of the microfilm reading machine and copier. Also to Goodnow Library Director Bill Talentino, research librarians Jennifer Ferris, Carolyn Anderson, Ann Shirly and Sheila Noah for providing quick and easy access to Town Reports and other documents.

Many residents of Sudbury not only consented to be interviewed, but also donated or loaned scrapbooks, old ledgers and other memorabilia. Hope Baldwin provided a list of old residents of The Town who were still living at press time; Leona Johnson allowed us to copy her family scrapbooks that date back to the Civil War and supported the project enthusiastically.

Joe Brown not only provided information on the Sudbury Industrial Development Commission, but loaned us personally taped interviews with several old-time residents now deceased, and rare 8 mm films of the Tercentenary celebration and life around Sudbury just prior to WWII. Ann Maker and Katherine Waters, daughters of Forrest Bradshaw, made available their father's scrapbook and other information on the reorganization of the Sudbury Proprietee as well as old letters and other documents in the Bradshaw-Rogers collection.

Clarence Ames shared his memories of the Ku Klux Klan's activities in Sudbury including the riot of 1925. Ed Kreitsek gave valuable insight on Sudbury's growing pains in the '50s, '60s, and early '70s as well as information on his antique apple orchard on Dudley Road and the Buddy Dog Humane Society.

Mildred Tallant shared her memories of the Old Town Hall fire in 1930 as well as her years as a teacher and children's librarian at the Goodnow Library. Barbara Deveneau and Natalie Eaton provided information on the 1938 hurricane and its aftermath, and John Bartlett provided copies of all the American Legion newsletters sent to Sudbury servicemen during WWII.

Rich Davison, Chairman of the Board of the Wayside Inn Corporation and a trustee for the Sudbury Foundation not only smoothed the way financially for the project, but read the final manuscript and caught several errors of omission and commission.

Former Selectmen John Taft and John Powers each provided his unique view on important events of the '70s and '80s and helped set me on the right path. Their wisdom and candor are appreciated.

My special thanks to the Sudbury Foundation, Sudbury Historical Society and the Wayside Inn Trustees for financing the project, and to the Sudbury Board of Selectmen for their support and permission to use art originally printed on town report covers during the '40s, '50s and '60s to illustrate the chapter headings.

The production staff of Berryville Press and Bill Mickelsen were heroic in pulling all the pieces together to create an outstanding finished product. Designer Anthony Villa's patience and skill were extraordinary as were the talents of Roger and Ron DeSaulniers of Rhault Die Cutting of Waltham who dusted off an ancient letterpress to print the line art from antique zinc plates. Toni Frederick, a historian in her own right, proofed the final draft and made some constructive suggestions as did Col. Jonathan F. "Bing" Swain, Bill Talentino, Richard Gnatowski and former Sudbury Town Manager Steve Ledoux. Fellow publisher Jameson Campagne shared his print contacts and offered valuable suggestions.

—Curtis F. Garfield

Introduction

When you take on the job of writing a sequel covering the last century in the history of an old town such as Sudbury you take on a thankless task, Everyone has their own opinion as to what's (or who's) important. Sudbury is a unique community filled with very active and opinionated people who aren't, and never have been, afraid to speak their minds or to stand up for what they believe.

So in writing this narrative I have chosen to concentrate on those events that have spurred people into action. Some of them are small, others monumental, still others controversial, but all "made the paper" in one fashion or another. Many had impact across the Commonwealth of Massachusetts.

Aside from one chapter about early education in the town, I have mentioned the Sudbury and Lincoln-Sudbury school systems only when they had an impact on the community as a whole. The history and metamorphosis of education in Sudbury is worthy of a book or thesis in itself.

This sequel is more of a story than a history. I have tried to give the reader a glimpse of what the town was like before the building booms of the '50s and '60s, and have included house numbers in the text wherever possible to help newcomers get their bearings. I have tried to explain not only what events took place, but why, and what impact they had on the community at the time.

No attempt has been made to cover up the warts and scars. There are at least two incidents documented here of the townspeople taking actions that may have denied certain individuals their civil rights, as well as a discussion of the meetings and cross burnings of the Knights of the Ku Klux Klan in which many prominent residents took part.

You'll find a great many names in these pages. I have included as many as possible because so many individuals--ranging from

Babe Ruth and Henry Ford to Bobby Moir, the caretaker of the Common--have had a hand in making Sudbury the unique place that it is. Rest assured that someone will get lost through the cracks, and for that sin of omission, I beg your forgiveness.

Sudbury is an unusual community. It is a town that gets under your skin after you've lived here a while. Once you've been a resident for any length of time, when someone asks where you hail from you'll always say "Sudbury" even if you're actually living someplace else. It's that kind of town.

—Curtis F. Garfield

"Some of E.W. Haynes Houses & Barns"

The late E. Helene Sherman, a nationally famous Medieval illustrator, made this sketch of the Loring Parsonage and its outbuildings from a very faint picture crayoned by A.S. Goodnow in 1876. The town purchased the property from the Haynes family after the old Town Hall burned in 1930 and used some of the land for the new Town Hall and the Center School.

The small house to the left of the Parsonage was destroyed in 1912 and the large barn facing the road was dismantled and rebuilt as headquarters for the highway department near the Town Pound on Concord Road. The other barn was moved to the Noyes property on Peakham Road.

I

A Quiet Country Town

In 1889, the South Sudbury Railroad Station was considered to be somewhat of a showpiece. It was only a year or so old, replacing an older depot that had burned to the ground two years before during a rash of unsolved railroad station fires. It stood at a junction of the new Massachusetts Central Line, which ran four round-trip commuter trains from Hudson to Boston daily, and the Lowell-Taunton Branch of the Old Colony Railway, which maintained a timetable of six passenger trains a day.

The depot had become a much busier place since the Massachusetts Central established passenger and freight service to Boston in 1881. Freight cars brought dry goods and flour from the city to George Hunt's general store and coal to fuel the boilers of the 15 greenhouse layouts scattered throughout the town. They returned with fruit, produce and flowers grown year-round under glass, unfinished furniture, casks and boxes and machine tools and parts.

The new station was shaped like an arrowhead, with a waiting room for each of the two lines on the sides, each heated by a pot-bellied stove capable of devouring huge chunks of firewood at a gulp. The station master's office overlooked the point where the two sets of tracks met.

Down past the waiting area, covered platforms protected the faded green-and-yellow, iron-wheeled carts loaded with sacks of mail and railway express packages. Across the tracks were sheds where heavy equipment could be loaded and unloaded efficiently and stored out of the weather.

The depot had once stood at the end of a lonely lane that ran up from the Post Road and skirted the upper end of the Parmenter Mill Pond, but now it was the southern terminus of Union Avenue, a modern thoroughfare built in 1879 to provide the shortest and straightest route to the junction of Meeting House (now Concord) and Old Lancaster Roads, and on to the town center.

On the morning of September 4, 1889, the new station was anything but a lonely place. It was decked out in red, white and blue bunting, as were many houses in town, and Station Road and Union Avenue were crowded with buggies, barges, horsemen and barking dogs as Chairman of the Day Jonas Hunt of Sudbury and his Wayland counterpart, R.T. Lombard, aided by Atherton W. Rogers and E.H. Atwood, tried desperately to organize the hodge-podge of horse-drawn conveyances into something resembling a line of march.

Musicians of the Fitchburg Military Band discreetly tuned up at one end of the station platform, hoping to avoid soiling their snappy dress uniforms with dust and horse manure before it was absolutely necessary. Small boys in straw hats and knee pants marched around in time to the music. It wasn't every day that a town celebrated a 250th birthday, or, as the *Sudbury Enterprise* called it, the "Quarter Millennial." [1]

A whistle from the direction of Parmenter's Mill signalled the return of a special Massachusetts Central train bearing the school children from Sudbury and Wayland who had gathered for ceremonies and a collation on the Wayland Town Common in the morning. Now the festivities in Sudbury could begin.

Hunt, the South Sudbury Postmaster and Town Clerk for many years, joined his committee in an open carriage to lead the way. His great shock of white whiskers reached to the first button on his greatcoat, nearly obscuring his dapper bow tie.

Hunt's carriage was followed by the band, playing patriotic airs under the direction of J.A. Platz and Drum Major Cyrus Roak, and a detachment from the Burnside Post No. 142 of the Grand Army of the Republic. Some of the old Civil War veterans chose to march under the command of E.A. Carter; others, too frail to walk the entire way, rode in one of two barges. Following two fire companies from Cochituate, came Captain D. W. Ricker at the head of 45 mounted cavalrymen in full uniform and a mounted Pequoit Indian unit under the command of Chief Spotted Thunder.

More decorated carriages carried Massachusetts State Treasurer G. A. Marden, President of the Day Homer Rogers, former Governor George S. Boutwell and Reverend Alfred Salerno Hudson, who had recently completed, at a cost of $3,000, a history of the town from 1638 "to the present day." A line of 30 more flower-decked carriages, containing citizens and guests, brought up the rear.

South Sudbury, according to Hudson, was the industrial and manufacturing section of the town and considered quite progressive. It consisted of: "a store, post office, machine shop, blacksmith shop, schoolhouse, chapel, grist mill, a junction depot, the Goodnow Library and 50 dwelling houses." Hunt's chosen line of march would pass almost all of them.

As the first units crossed the bridge above the millpond and headed east on the Boston Post Road, Hunt could plainly see the buildings of Mill Village, dominated by the machine shop of Rufus Hurlbut and Samuel Rogers. Hurlbut and Rogers turned out cutting-off lathes, engine governors and lathe chucks, and shipped them all over the country. Charles O. Parmenter's grist and saw mill, originally built by Peter Noyes in 1660, lay just below in the shadow of the dam. John Garfield's wheelwright and blacksmith's shop occupied a separate frame building across the mill yard.

Not far away to the west was Hubbard Brown's range of cucumber greenhouses. Since his facility was built in 1879, fourteen other farmers had taken up the trade and now more than 100,000 square feet of land was under glass, requiring nearly 800 tons of coal yearly to fire the boilers. Brown's competition had expanded to grow lettuce, rhubarb, tomatoes and flowers—primarily carnations—in addition to the popular "cukes."

Down the road a few more yards, a crowd had gathered in front of George W. Hunt's new general store and post office at the corner of Concord Road. The old store had burned in 1887 under mysterious circumstances, (a local newspaper correspondent claimed it was torched by "one of the Hanlan boys" whose brother had been wounded in an 1887 burglary attempt and later died). [2] Hunt had rebuilt immediately, noting that his family had been doing business on that corner for more than 75 years.

Up the street, on the left, the octagon-shaped library building, built with funds donated by John Goodnow, stood at the near end of its long, narrow mall lined with young maple trees. Diagonally across the street, the new Congregational Church building was in the final stages of construction. It stood on the old site of the Wadsworth Academy—this had burned down ten years before when young Seneca Hall, who was to go on to become Sudbury's chief of police for 43 years, tried to smoke a skunk out of the cellar. [3]

Near the top of Green Hill, Mount Wadsworth Cemetery and its monument, which the town had only recently adopted as its official seal, loomed through the trees. On this spot Captain Samuel Wadsworth and 28 of his men had died defending the Massachusetts Bay Colony against attack by King Philip of Pokonoket and his braves on April 21, 1676. Hunt recalled the dedication ceremonies 37 years before, held during a blinding snowstorm.

Across the road from the cemetery entrance stood the home of Israel How Brown, an important stop on the Underground Railroad that smuggled fugitive slaves to Canada. Hunt remembered wheelwright John Garfield showing him Brown's hay wagon with secret compartments built into the bed. A little discomfort was a small price to pay for freedom, he thought.

The crowds beside the road grew larger as the procession moved past the Music Hall which stood opposite the intersection with Goodman's Hill Road. The old building had been used for services by the Congregationalists who would soon abandon it as their new chapel in South Sudbury was nearly finished.

Just up the road past the blacksmith shop, the pillared front porch of the general store, run by John W. Garfield and his son-in-law, William M Parmenter, was crowded with excited people. Youngsters waved tiny flags and cheered through the windows of the schoolroom on the third floor where, one day, a distant Garfield cousin named James Abram Garfield would be schoolmaster and, later, President of the United States..

Further on, J.L. Willis's store (today's Hosmer House) was also jammed with spectators. The crowds spilled over to the First

Parish Church and Methodist Church lawns and around in front
of the two-story former Center District Schoolhouse. In two years
this building would become the Grange Hall.

Many of the spectators had driven in from farms in North
Sudbury and their rigs filled the horse sheds beside the Church.
Edwin Conant's general store and post office was the center of
what passed for a village in North Sudbury—no more than a few
houses, farms and a district school scattered along the Fitchburg
Turnpike.

There were fewer houses in Sudbury Center Village, perhaps 30
or so plus the blacksmith shop, a new school, two stores, the
church and the Town Hall. These residents had come on foot.
Those who didn't have tickets to the catered luncheon brought
bulging picnic hampers and blankets. Most of the men wore
locally-made, wide-brimmed Panama straw hats while the
women showed off their calico dresses and sunbonnets made of
straw and lined with cloth. Many of the little girls wore sunbonnets and aprons over their dresses to stave off the filth on the
roads.

The $1-a-plate dinner at the Town Hall attracted 600 guests, 100
more than Algernon Jones had bargained for, but the Waltham
caterer and his staff were equal to the occasion. After the meal
the crowd, now some 2,000 strong, jockeyed for positions in the
shade in front of a reviewing stand, "handsomely" decorated by
Raymond Kennedy of Hudson, to listen to orations by Homer
Rogers, Historian A.S. Hudson, and many other dignitaries.
Mercifully, most of the speeches were short, witty, and inter-
spersed with musical numbers by the band. [4]

As the sun set over Mount Nobscot, the Maynard Brass Band
tuned up for an evening of music as multi-colored paper lanterns
glowed around the Common. Fireworks and illuminations punc-
tuated the night sky.

Hunt, Hurlbut, Rogers and Edwin A. Powers joined Hudson on
the steps of the Town Hall and looked out over the scene. "What
would Sudbury be like 50 or 100 years from now?" someone wondered. Would there be drastic changes? Would businessmen still
ride the trains to work in Boston, and would agriculture and

greenhouses continue to be the major industries? After all, Sudbury had grown very little in the last 100 years.

All agreed that there would be some changes. Life is constant change, everybody knew that--but what would happen to their quiet country town in the next 100 years would be beyond their comprehension.

The Sudbury Minuteman

Erected "In honor of the soldiers and sailors of Sudbury who fought at Lexington, Concord, Bunker Hill and other battles of the Revolutionary War 1775-1783," the Minuteman statue stands on land owned by the First Parish Church at the gateway to Mount Pleasant Cemetery.

Dedicated on June 17, 1896, the monument cost $2,500 which included the statue and grading and preparation of the site. Costs were underwritten by Joanna Gleason, a retired school teacher, and by the town. The minuteman is seven feet tall and stands on a 10-foot pedestal of Quincy granite. Weight of the monument is estimated at about 20 tons. (Illustration by King Coffin)

II

Joanna Gleason's Gift

The Committee to oversee the erection of a monument to honor the memory of Sudbury's Revolutionary War soldiers found itself in a bind that would become quite familiar to future generations of town officials. After consultations with well-known architect Mr. A.F. Haynes, it had approved a $2,000 monument of the best Quincy granite, only to discover that there was only $1,500 in funds available to pay for it. [1]

Chairman of the Board of Selectmen Nahum Goodnow of South Sudbury was particularly embarrassed. On June 17, 1895, his board had gratefully accepted the generous gift of $500 from Joanna Gleason, "the same to be expended by the town in the erection of a monument to the memory of the soldiers of the town of Sudbury in the Revolutionary War; provided, however, that the same amount, or a greater one, be expended by the town in the erection of the same monument within one year from the acceptance of this offer." (Signed) Joanna Gleason.

The Special Town Meeting called on that date not only passed a resolution accepting the gift, but pledged $1,000 of town funds to allow the project to go forward. A committee consisting of Selectmen Goodnow, Waldo L. Stone, and Samuel Underwood, together with Town Clerk Jonas S. Hunt, and George E. Harrington was chosen to select a site and design and supervise the construction of the monument.

A small, rocky lot near the entrance to Mount Pleasant Cemetery, controlled by the First Parish Church, was selected. The church gave its blessing in writing, and, after reviewing a large number of designs, the committee commissioned A.F. Haynes to create a work to its specifications. The only problem that remained was to find the remaining $500 to complete the project. Hunt, the Clerk of the Committee, takes up the story during his remarks at the dedication ceremony on June 17, 1896: "Just at this time, however, a second communication was received from Mrs. Gleason, accompanied by an additional gift of five hundred dollars, which, of course, relieved the committee at once. Whether Mrs. Gleason had learned of the dilemma of the committee or preferred to share the expense equally with the town, I am not able to say."

The chances are that Mrs. Gleason wanted to assure that a proper memorial to Sudbury's Revolutionary soldiers was erected. The communication accompanying her second donation specified that the structure was to be rendered "one of more artistic and heroic proportions." Her grandfather, Captain Timothy Adams, helped defend Bunker Hill and her father, Major Jonas Parker, defended Fort Warren in Boston Harbor against the British during the War of 1812 and joined Daniel Webster and the Marquis de LaFayette at the laying of the Bunker Hill Monument cornerstone, June 17, 1825.

"Being myself the granddaughter of a Soldier of the Revolution, who was one of the earliest in service of his country, and who kept the field as long as his bodily strength allowed, I have an especial personal reason for desiring to perpetuate the memory of all those patriots who, like him, risked everything for the cause of freedom," she wrote in her letter expressing regrets that she would be unable to attend the dedication ceremonies.

"As a resident of this good old town of Sudbury, I remember that her sons did their full duty in the great war for independence from that first memorable day at Concord until the last British soldier quitted the soil of America," she recalled. " My ancestor, from the town of my birth [Carlisle] and your ancestors, from the town where I have lived for so many years, alike in patriotism and courage, stood together at Bunker Hill one hundred and twenty one years ago, and it is their deeds and their devotion that you will commemorate upon the anniversary of that day and that the statue you will then unveil will always keep fresh in the memories of Sudbury's children to the latest time."

With all financial obstacles removed, the site was cleared and graded and crews from Badger Brothers of West Quincy began the work of erecting the monument itself, a Quincy granite pedestal surmounted by a heroic-proportioned figure of a

Revolutionary soldier carved in Westerly, Rhode Island, granite. The monument stands seventeen feet high and weighs more than 19 tons.

Work was completed in plenty of time for the committee to organize dedication ceremonies on Bunker Hill Day, 1896, with more than a thousand people on hand to hear an oration by the Honorable John L. Bates of Boston and addresses by President of the Day Homer Rogers, Jonas Hunt, Town Historian Alfred Salerno Hudson and others. Miss Mary Edith Goodnow, daughter of Nahum Goodnow, who later became Mary Goodnow Cutler of East Sudbury, and Miss Alice Esther Bent, both descendants of Revolutionary War soldiers, unveiled the monument.

The monument was far from being the first example of Joanna Gleason's largesse to her adopted town. Born in Carlisle in 1819, she attended Carlisle and Concord public schools as well as Lexington, Billerica and Westford Academies. She went on to teach in Concord and Billerica schools and was very proud of a teacher's certificate dated April 30, 1836, which was signed by Ralph Waldo Emerson, at that time Chairman of the Concord School Committee.

She married John Gleason on April 11, 1858, and the couple soon developed a reputation for providing financial support for various institutions not only in Sudbury, but in Concord and Carlisle as well. A year after her husband died in 1879, she slipped on some ice and injured a hip that required the use of a crutch the rest of her life. She still managed to make frequent trips to Boston on the train to see to her financial affairs. In 1890, a heavy piece of metal fell on her foot and for the last seven years of her life she was bedridden with bone cancer.

Although Mrs. Gleason did not make a habit of calling on the needy, her aid was rarely sought in vain, and her private deeds of charity accomplished as much good as did her public donations. "Few really understood her," said the Sudbury correspondent for the *Lowell Weekly Journal*. "While a natural dignity was hers, no pride ever defaced it. She was endowed with a keen insight, a clear judgement, was quick to read character, and keen to see and distrust anything false. She showed not by words, but by her daily life that she felt that her powers, advantages and possessions were only trusts committed to her keeping, of which she must one day give an account."

Mrs. Gleason may well have been aware that the day of reckoning was not very far off when she set a deadline of June 17, 1896 for the completion of the work. She was unable to attend the dedication ceremonies on that date and died on October 16, 1896.

"She loved life and leaves saddened hearts behind her," read the obituary in the *Lowell Weekly Journal*. "We can all echo the lines inscribed on her monument: "A blessing's gone, a noble form is riven. To darken this cold earth and gladden heaven."

Even with her life slowly slipping away, Joanna Gleason managed time for one last act of generosity. Upon hearing that funds were needed to complete landscaping at the Memorial, she donated another $100 to the town.

Less than a month after the dedication, Samuel B. Rogers, perhaps inspired by the Revolutionary War Memorial, donated $2,000 for a Civil War memorial statue in South Sudbury with the proviso that the statue be dedicated on Memorial Day, 1897 and that the expense of the foundation and dedication not be appropriated by the town. The site selected was in front of the recently-enlarged Goodnow Library.

Not long after the Civil War Monument's dedication, "Reno," a correspondent for the *Lowell Weekly Journal* voiced his approval.

"Let the added glories of the town in the shape of new monuments be associated with the high art of modern embellishment and let the grounds around them be laid out and cared for with an aesthetic taste that is in accord with these beautiful memorials, but let the objects of a century back remind one of their day and its customs and people; and although the rank grass does flourish in its wildness about the moss-grown tombstones and although the ground may be uplifted and thrown askew by the frosts of successive years, these may only serve to give interest to the stranger who strolls about Sudbury to find in it some vestiges of a town of the long ago..."

"Reno" would be pleased to know that strangers still stroll about Sudbury and soak in the Town's history, but today they not only come from the neighboring communities, but from all over the world. Thanks to the generosity of Joanna Gleason and Samuel B. Rogers, the bravery of the sons and daughters of Sudbury will never be forgotten.

Redstone School

Henry Ford discovered this building being used as a storage shed behind the Sterling Baptist Church in 1926, bought it for $35 and had it torn down and rebuilt near the Wayside Inn. Barely six months later, on January 17, 1927, 16 Sudbury children, including Tom Winship who would later become the editor of The Boston Globe, *were matriculating there with Ford paying the bills.*

The school graduated its last class in June of 1951. Among the students was Earl Meader, the son of Eleanor Stone Meader who was one of the school's original students 25 years before.

The building stood for 60 years on Redstone hill in Sterling where Mary Sawyer made it famous by bringing her lamb to school and provoking a controversy over the author of the well-known nursery rhyme which still persists today.

14

III

Sudbury Gets Serious About Schools

The early '90s had brought other changes to Sudbury, many of them in the schools. The town had always had its share of residents who ran businesses in Boston, but now wealthy people from the city were buying up land and erecting elaborate homes. It was apparent that Sudbury's system of district schoolhouses was rapidly becoming out of date.

In 1889, school expenses amounted to $2,713, including salaries for eight teachers, supplies, and maintenance of district school buildings scattered throughout the town. Veteran schoolmistresses Lucie K. Welch and Leonara K. Battles earned premium wages of $13 a week, while the rest of the staff earned $9. The tax rate that year was $10 per thousand. [1]

Debate had been raging for some time over the advantages and disadvantages of a central school house. Proponents pointed to a savings in teacher salaries, better supervision and curriculum, and less heating and maintenance costs. Opponents countered that the district schools cut down on transportation costs and time while still providing an adequate education.

The controversy came to a head at the 1890 Town Meeting where the town voted to "procure a suitable site and build a new schoolhouse in the Center District." The Selectmen quickly moved to purchase the estate of the late Elisha Haynes, a piece of property once owned and farmed by the Reverend Israel Loring who was the town's first minister west of the Sudbury River. Seven thousand dollars was set aside for the cost of the land and a four-room building, with another $2,000 earmarked for furniture and heat. [2]

Expenses for the new building came in $372.52 under budget at $8,627.48, including $485.80 for boilers (which later were found faulty and required replacement), $117.87 to J.H. Hammett of Boston for slate blackboards, and $292.20 for school desks and chairs for two rooms.

Less than a year later, the School Committee hailed the new four-room building as "Large enough for the entire school population of the town as now constituted." That building still exists today as the four front rooms of the Flynn Town Office Building on Old Sudbury Road.

The School Committee soon discovered that building a central school was one thing, but getting parents to send their children there was quite another. On April 6, 1891, the town directed the Committee to "appoint a superintendent of schools and consolidate all district schools in the new schoolroom(s) in the center district by the beginning of next fall term." That vote was rescinded at a Special Town Meeting on May 4, and THAT vote was in turn reversed on June 22.

Not to be outdone, voters at another Special Town Meeting on October 12, appropriated $2,500 for a new schoolhouse in the Landham school district. The building stood at the junction of Landham Road and the Boston Post Road and was moved in 1920 to Massasoit Avenue where it became part of the South School. [3]

The sparring continued in the spring of 1892 when a Town Meeting vote once again authorized the School Committee to employ a superintendent of schools and bring about district cooperation if advisable. In the same session, the town voted to establish a High School program starting that fall. Five hundred dollars was appropriated to furnish a High School room at the new school building in Sudbury Center, and Mr. A.F. Haynes of Watertown donated a Howard clock. [4]

Sudbury's population was small enough that the Town wasn't required to build and maintain a High School. Only 60 towns in Massachusetts maintained one in the 1890s. Students wishing a secondary education were sent to high schools in Waltham or Framingham.

Edward J. Cox was engaged as the new superintendent of schools with additional duties as principal of the high school. Thirty-four children, divided into classes of 13 and 21 pupils respectively, started classes in the fall of 1892. Classes ran from 9 a.m. to 1 p.m. Monday through Thursday and an extra hour on Friday. Twenty-nine grammar school children opted for advanced grammar school at the Center building rather than remain in the district schools.

The High School issue had been a topic of discussion since 1888. Letters to the editor of the *Lowell Weekly Journal* of November 19, 1888 from Sarah Pratt warned that too much high school education would: "lead too often to a self-satisfaction that is a bar to future progress."

Pratt suggested: "Lengthening of the grammar school course and spending the time that would be employed half learning languages such as Latin or French in acquiring by well-directed observation an interest in and knowledge of natural science and a taste, by carefully guided reading, for history, biography and geography which shall be sources of inspiration and happiness through life and that shall reject, with mental nausea the trashy second-rate fiction that makes [up] so large a part of our public library."

Other opponents of a new high school for Sudbury worried that the town could not afford to pay enough in salary to keep a qualified teacher from moving on to greener pastures. They suggested instead that the town award two or three annual scholarships by competitive examination which should be enough to pay the tuition at a good high school in a neighboring town.

Critics who claimed that Sudbury would be unable to keep a qualified superintendent at a yearly salary of $800 proved to be correct. In 1897, Harrison G. Fay replaced Cox and was in turn replaced by Frank O. Jones who immediately demanded the school committee hire two assistant superintendents or establish a district superintendency. [5]

Fay was re-appointed superintendent in June of 1897 and recommended adding two new grades to the grammar school and lengthening the school year. The School Committee, mindful that many of the children were needed to help with farm work in the summer, set it at 37 weeks.

The Superintendent controversy came to a head at the 1898

Town Meeting where, facing an enrollment of 219 students in seven different schools and a payroll of nine teachers, the taxpayers approved a joint superintendency agreement with the towns of Wayland and Dover. The School Committee filled the position with Rufus E. Corlew at a salary of $1,500 a year and, in what many considered a controversial decision, hired Miss Grace Parker as the first female principal of the high school. [6]

Slowly, but surely, the committee was breaking down local opposition to a centralized school system. The Pratt District School was moved to Sudbury center and attached to the rear of the Center School, allowing the addition of an eighth grade for the first time. The 1901 town meeting made it official, voting to transport intermediate grammar and high school students to the Center School.

In the meantime school expenses were creeping up. By 1899, $6,588.31 had been appropriated. That dropped to $5,800 in 1900 despite the addition of "an advanced laboratory containing two magnificent tables seldom seen in towns the size of Sudbury, one for physical sciences and one for chemistry." [7] (These tables were still there in the 1950s) By the 1901 Town Meeting, school expenses had ballooned to $7,207, $850.12 of which was defrayed by a one-time grant from the Massachusetts School Fund.

Even as the quality of the schools improved, the administration found itself facing another problem. During his last year as school committee chairman, Frank Barton complained that the curriculum was educating the children away from the farms and away from Sudbury. "Everything they have learned here leads them away to the larger cities and towns. Why not teach them some of the branches of horticulture? Why not greenhousing or the study of forestry? One can go a long way to find a town that has as much white pine as Sudbury."

A lot of that pine got burned in woodstoves all over Sudbury during the winter of 1901-02, which was so cold that the library was open only on Saturdays. To make matters worse, it was discovered that the heating contractors for the Center School building had failed to install the sheet iron and asbestos liner on one of the boilers, necessitating the use of wood stoves throughout the building. It eventually cost the town $2,249.30 to get the problem corrected. [8]

Meanwhile, J.T. Corlew, Rufus Corlew's son, had assumed control of Superintendency Union No. 30, and was taking every step he could to save the town money. He extended the length of the school year to 40 weeks in order to qualify for a state bounty of $300 and proposed raising the roof of the ell on the Center School to accommodate a room for fifth graders. The Sudbury High School class of 04 would become the first to take 13 years of schoolwork before earning a diploma.

Corlew retired in favor of S.C. Hutchinson in 1907, but the clamor for more practical education continued. Hutchinson recommended that: "Sudbury children should be educated for Sudbury. The boys to be intelligent farmers and the girls intelligent homemakers." He also asked for higher teacher salaries. He was replaced by Charles F. Pryor a year later.

The trend toward more practical education in Sudbury schools was an ongoing theme up until the beginning of WWI. An article in the 1908 town meeting to close the high school and replace it with a manual training school was defeated, but Town Meeting did establish a committee to investigate the education of the children in the high school grades and make recommendations at the next Town Meeting.

In 1911 there were 15 teachers in the Sudbury system, earning a collective $5,357.44. Out of the total enrollment of 202 children, 34 matriculated in the high school. There were five graduates of the class of 1911 including Harvey Fairbank, who would go on to a life of faithful service to his town. [9]

Superintendent Frank H. Benedict finally took action on the curriculum in 1912. Greek was dropped altogether and Latin and other subjects were placed on trial against courses in practical arts, business and woodworking. Solid geometry was offered to boys only and the commercial law course was put forward to the 11th and 12th grades. An economics course was also offered.

"There is a desire for more practical subjects in high school as only six to ten percent of the children will go on to college," he said in his 1912 report to the town.

Despite the fact that Sudbury High School enjoyed great respect among Ivy League college registrars, keeping a staff together continued to be a problem. Benedict reported in 1913 that half his staff was new and, five years later, reported to the School Committee that the town would have to increase salaries on the average of $200 per teacher in order to be competitive.

Benedict, in his ninth year as superintendent, reminded the committee that, starting in 1919, the state required that full-time teachers be compensated at the rate of no less than $550 for the school year--about $100 more than Sudbury teachers were earning. He also pointed out that normal school graduates were starting at between $600 and $700 and that teachers of any ability were in short supply. At the end of 1919 only Mrs. Pickett and four other teachers were being compensated at more than the minimum and the School Committee asked for a budget of $15,100, $8,500 of which was for teacher salaries.

Benedict would serve the town as superintendent for 33 years and in that time would see teacher salaries rise to nearly $2,000 annually. One wonders what he would think of the compensation paid to educators today.

In 1927, Benedict hired a young, World War I veteran to the position of Principal of the High School. Alan F. Flynn went on to become one of the most beloved educators in the history of the town. The Flynn Town Office Building was named in his honor shortly after his death in 1976.

"There never was a discipline problem in Al Flynn's administration," Selectman Harvey Fairbank was to say. "No strong-arm tactics either. The students had great respect for him and always knew he meant what he said."

Besides schools, alcohol trafficking occupied the minds of Sudbury citizens of the '90s. In 1892, the *Lowell Weekly Journal* reported that "Selectman George A. Haynes and constables Bent and Barton made a raid on the premises of Rosa

Blanchard of North Sudbury who has been suspected of familiarity with bad spirits. It was evident upon entering the house, that the occupant had been warned, and, although plenty of kegs, jugs, bottles etc. were found, all were empty.

> "After a thorough search of the house, the party made a tour of the farm and came upon a woodchuck's burrow that looked 'a little suspicious,' " they reported. "When closely examined the burrow was found to contain a five-gallon keg of whisky enclosed in a bag. This was taken away and the party adjourned. Further developments are expected." [11]

Four years later, the 1896 Town Meeting appropriated $200 for the "detection, prosecution and conviction of liquor sellers," and encouraged town officers and officials to use all the power in their command to convict them.

Moonshining wasn't the only crime to keep Deputy Chief of Police Seneca W. Hall busy. George Hunt's store in South Sudbury was burglarized, with the thief leaving his old suit of clothes in return for a new one. A large quantity of canned goods was also taken.

The Wayside Inn changed hands twice during the '90s. Atherton W. Rogers, ex-Mayor Herbert Howe of Marlborough and ex-Alderman Homer Rogers of Boston bought it from Lucy A. Newton in 1893. Mrs. Newton had inherited it from the estate of Lyman Howe. The *Lowell Weekly Journal* speculated that Ex-Mayor Howe's interest in the 90-acre property stemmed from his connection with a proposed new state central electric plan that would include an electric railroad from Waltham to Marlborough. Plans called for that railway to pass directly in front of the Inn.

In 1897, Malden Wool Merchant Edward R. Lemon read about the Inn in the *New England Magazine*, drove out to inspect it, bought it on the spot, and, on April 1, 1897, opened it to the public once more.

Lemon moved a woodshed to the east end of the building and converted it into an art gallery and museum for his collection of antique furniture. He enlarged the third floor of the main building and added dormer windows in the front, prompting one local correspondent to the Journal to bemoan the passing of the "good old days."

> "...Few and far between are the relics of even old Sudbury becoming so far as concerns relics that retain much of their originality. In the past year, or two years, change has been busy in this historic township. The last picture of the "Wayside Inn" gives that ancient hostelry an air unlike what surrounded it when the scroll read: 'By the Name of Howe'."

> "No ghosts would enter the newly-made porch or peer from the modern made windows. The old Walker Garrison House has become an ash heap, a destiny that befell many another farm dwelling in the days of the town's early history.

> "The terminal part of the old Hop Brook Road to Marlborough has become, since summer, a 'state highway.' The road over Sand Hill has become a boulevard and, one by one, the district schoolhouses are disappearing with all their local influence and associations.

> "But enough has been said to suffice the object of showing the importance of preserving what things of old remain in their primitive condition." 12

There was another significant purchase in Sudbury that year. The Reverend Edwin Hosmer arrived in town with his wife and four children and bought the James Willis house and store on the corner of Concord and Old Sudbury Roads for $1. One of his daughters was Florence Armes Hosmer who would live in that house until she died at the age of 98 in 1978.

Henry Ford had yet to visit Sudbury in the early 1900s, but the motor cars he built were rapidly becoming a nuisance. The April 18, 1904 Town Meeting instructed the Selectmen to do something about the speeding autos on the streets of the town and appropriated $100 in expense money.

Special Police Officer P.J. McManus billed the town for 20 days' service, use of horse and car and expenses, less court fees of $31.63 including $1.25 for repair of his stop watch. F.F. Gerry, an attorney, was engaged to try 23 speeding cases and was paid $100. By the end of the year, $682.42 had been spent in the enforcement of motor vehicle laws.

First Parish Church

The building we see today was raised in 1797 at the cost of $6,025.93 when George Washington was president. It replaced a smaller building built in 1724 after the Reverend Israel Loring accepted the call to be the town's first minister west of the Sudbury River.

Sunday worship was broken into morning and afternoon segments with a break for lunch in between. An hourglass was used to time the sermon lest the minister become too long winded. The building was unheated and some of the congregation brought in their dogs to help warm their feet during cold winter Sundays.

Nineteenth Century Sudbury

To the left of this picture, created by Lubin Doucette from a 19th Century print, is Parmenter's general store which was shortly there-after purchased and moved by Henry Ford to Marlborough to become the Wayside Country Store. Also no longer in existence is the Old Town Hall which burned in February of 1930.

The First Parish Church building was constructed in 1797. It is joined to the Town Hall by the carriage sheds which were used by the town during the week and the church on Sundays. The clock in the steeple was once the property of the town, which paid for its winding and any needed repairs.

IV

A Ride With Uncle Atherton Rogers

We children are sitting on the wooden steps of the Sudbury Town Hall this October morning of 1917, waiting for a special treat. Uncle Atherton Rogers has promised us a ride in his old Democrat wagon to show us the town as he remembered it sixty years ago when he was our age. Uncle Atherton is a successful businessman in Boston and has invested much of his wealth in the town. He lives in a big house called "Hilltops" on the hill behind the new Memorial Congregational Church in South Sudbury. [1]

The sun is flashing from the weathervane of the First Parish Church which some people have said looks like Mrs. Loring's bloomers hung out to dry, and the maples along the roadway are a riot of red and gold with streaks of green mixed in.

There's Uncle Atherton now. He's not our real uncle, but everybody calls him that, just the way they used to do to Uncle Johnny Goodnow of East Sudbury who lived to be more than 100 years old. It is a term of respect.

"Come sit on the high seat where you can hear and see, children," he invites as he walks the horses to the watering trough for a drink. "I will start by telling you about things here at the Center and work around the town.

"At the Center years ago were located all the churches," he tells us. "Also the Town Hall--as it still is. The First Parish or Unitarian, Methodist and Orthodox were here. The school house for that district was very close to the Methodist Church. For a few years, a new building for school purposes has taken its place and has the different grades to high school in it. The old building is owned and occupied by the Sudbury Grange.

"The Town Hall is as it was as I first remember it. The Orthodox Society moved from its old quarters in 1891 to South Sudbury into a new building and is now called the Memorial

Congregational Church. The first storekeepers I can remember here were Smith, Jones, Burbeck and Willis. Then Jonas S. Hunt, John Garfield, Edwin A. Powers, and the present owner, Mr. William M. Parmenter.

"The oldest cemetery and the newest are close together here, separated only by the street. One dates back to the early 1600s and the other a good many years later. The old tombs still are where they were built and judging from their condition, will remain for years to come."

Uncle Atherton glances around the common once more, ticking off the familiar buildings of his youth.

"Sewall Taylor and Jonas Tower were the wheelwrights for many years. Taylor's shop is still standing [285 Concord Road], but he has gone over the river. The Hurlbut Parsonage [233 Concord Road] and the Bigelow [254 Old Sudbury Road] are still standing and are as good to look upon as ever. They were made to withstand the storms of many years.

"The buildings haven't changed, but the familiar faces are few. Wheeler Haynes was a familiar figure in the Center. For years he transported milk from the different farms to Cambridge. Webster Moore kept a small hotel in the house now occupied by Walter Stone [301 Concord Road]. When the Sudbury Rifle Co. paraded on old election day, his place was very attractive.

"Assabet, now Maynard, was part of Sudbury then and on town meeting days the old hall would be crowded with poll tax payers from the mill if that village wanted anything special. Now Maynard is a thrifty manufacturing town by itself.

"Sudbury is on the map with its two lines of railroads, telephone, telegraph and electric lights in houses as well as on its streets. It also has a private school, the Whiting School for Girls [now Featherland Park]."

The horses are rested and watered so it is time to start our ride. Uncle Atherton turns the team toward the road to Concord, past the Revolutionary War Memorial, the Revolutionary and

Mt. Pleasant Cemeteries, the tombs and hearse house and over the hill to a large country estate owned by famous architect Ralph Adams Cram.

"A fine old country home made doubly so by Mr. Cram who has added to its beauty with some changes," says Uncle Atherton. "Nearby he has erected a stone church of pretty design and has services there during the summer months when he occupies his lovely home. It is of the Episcopal denomination." [This is today's St. Elizabeth's Chapel].

We pass along by good farms belonging to Bents, Hunts and Haynes, all descended from Sudbury's old families, and finally come to a flatiron-shaped piece of land where the roads split, one turning right to Concord and the other bearing left to North Sudbury and Maynard.

"Here stood the old Pantry Schoolhouse, where the Bents, Hunts, Puffers, Haynes, Bartons, Lomasneys, Dewise and others got their first training as scholars," says Uncle Atherton. "This old building has been moved away."

He steers the team down the left fork, and soon we pass the old North Sudbury railroad station and the cemetery and turn left on the old North Road from Boston to Lancaster and points west. Uncle Atherton tells us that Nahum Thompson once had a small store near here, but it has been closed for many years.

"Let's turn back by Uncle Leander Haynes and Captain Jones' places," he suggests. "At the beginning of the Civil War, 1861, I went to a flag raising at Capt. Jones [Barton Farm on what is now called Liberty Ledge]. The Sudbury Rifles and the Sudbury Brass Band were there, and it was a great afternoon for us boys. A good many of the old rifle company enlisted in the 13th Mass Volunteers. Some never returned alive, but they were brave and protected the flag as long as they had life."

We pass on, going through what Uncle Atherton calls the Perry District [out today's Marlboro Road, down Fairbank Road and Dutton Road. The Perry place was the Atkinson farmhouse previously owned by Babe Ruth].

"We remember Billy Moore's cider mill near Capt. Jim's. It was afterwards owned by my father, then by Edwin Gerry, then by Nathan Pratt and by his estate at present," he says. "Down through the woods [the length of today's Pratt Mill Road] a mile or so we find another mill owned by Charles Haynes, known today as Willis Mill. Each mill did grinding and sawing and sold grain."

We go by the old Noyes and Hayden places [following Peakham Road south] by the old Walker Farm out on to the Marlboro Road [Route 20] and head west toward the Wayside Inn, made famous by Longfellow's book of poems of the same name. Uncle Atherton ties his sweating team within reach of the watering trough near the door and we get down, walk around and look at the buildings while the horses drink.

"This was called the Red Horse Tavern in my boyhood," He recalls. "This style of building was common along all the main roads of Massachusetts. The old inn had 18 rooms. The rooms had fireplaces and were low with the big beams encased and sides sheathed up part way from the floor.

"Squire Howe [Lyman Howe, the last Howe innkeeper] was there and had a housekeeper and Buckley Parmenter was the man of all work. The old bar room could tell of wonderful times if it could speak. I purchased the Inn in 1893 of Mrs. Newton, who was one of the original Howes, for ex-Mayor S. Herbert Howe of Marlboro and Hon. Homer Rogers of Boston, a Sudbury boy.

"I had charge of the place one season and we changed the old driveway barn so that the hill in front of the house might be seen. Parties from Marlboro, Framingham, Concord and other places would come and dance in the old hall, and Mr. Seymour and I would set the tables and serve the lunch they would bring with them. We had tables, chairs, linen, crockery, but no food, only what was brought by parties.

"Over the old bar we served soft drinks and cigars. We also had things to sell with the cut [picture] of the house on them and also the book, *'The Tales of a Wayside Inn.'* Over 4,000 registered between May and December. People from all over the world. Today Mr. [Edward R.] Lemon has it beautifully fixed up and it is one of the showplaces for the state and country.

"Just above is the nail and tack factory and home of J.C. Howe which is now owned by William Bright [The Calvin Howe house burned down during the Ford era and the mill was dismantled after the Wayside Inn grist mill was completed in 1929]."

Uncle Atherton unties the team after one last draught of cool well water that we have helped to pump, and we head east along the Boston Post Road toward South Sudbury. Soon we pass the old Peakham district school and the old Bacon homestead [566 Boston Post Road] on the left, where he takes up his narrative once more.

"Mrs. Bacon lived to be 102 or thereabout, a fine old lady. Mr. Bacon lived to a ripe old age as well, but I've forgotten how old. The Osgoods now own the place and have remodeled it quite a bit. Here on the left is the Stone place which was a hotel, I was told, but not in my day.

"Now we come to Bonnie Brook Farm [now Raytheon Corp]. Mr. Borden has three farms, some 150 cows, milking machines and every convenience for feeding and watering, carriers for the fertilizers, rooms for cooling and separating the milk and cream, and washing machine for bottles. He makes cheese, butter and ice cream in season. He has a tea room and everything on quite a large scale. It is now owned by H.P. Hood and Sons and is doing a large business."

On the right side of the street, we pass the greenhouses of Harland Rogers and James Tulis who grow carnations to be shipped by rail to markets all over the northeast. A little farther along we clatter across the tracks of the New York, New Haven and Hartford Railroad and later on the Central Mass branch of the Boston and Maine.

As we cross the bridge over Wash Brook above Parmenter's Mill and pass by the machine shop of Hurlbut, Rogers and Co., Uncle Atherton tells us that the stream now supports four mills. At one time it supported seven: Hager's in Marlboro, Howe's near the Wayside Inn, Knight-Dutton on Dutton Road, Moore's (Pratt's), also on Dutton Road, Conners and Willis on Peakham Road, and the Richardson Mill in South Sudbury which was later purchased by Charles O. Parmenter.

"There's not a log in the old Mill Lane anymore," he says wistfully. "What times we boys had playing and hiding in and around them! In the rear of this old mill were the factories of S.B. Rogers & Co., manufacturers of leatherboards, shoe stiffings and box toes. That business has moved to Maine, but the Hurlbut-Rogers Machine Company is still going and is a busy plant. The overseas war [WWI] has made it so."

We stop in front of the large house [today's Sudbury Professional Building, which still retains the configuration of the old tavern] nearly at the corner of Boston Post Road and Concord Road which Uncle Atherton tells us was once a busy tavern. "The proprietor, I remember, was Samuel Fessenden," he says. "It had two big driveways and places for horses. Loads of hay, furniture or anything bulky could get in the barn as the entrance was high and very wide. The stalls for the horses were for two horses together.

"The tavern was a big square building connected with the barn by a big shed. I have been over the house many times since it was closed as a hotel. The office and bar room were the most attractive parts."

We leave the horses drinking at the water trough erected by Mr. Goodnow and follow Uncle Atherton across the busy intersection. He points out a large square building with huge windows overlooking Mill Lane. "The old Kidder shoe shop," he says. "Handmade shoes and boots and they would look ancient and honorable today. We got a good deal for our money in those days. Capt. Kidder is gone, the old hotel and big barns torn down...."

We cross again and investigate Hunt's general store on the opposite corner. George W. Hunt is the owner but is in ill health so George Grover is running things. Uncle Atherton tells us what it was like when he was a boy and Gardner and Luther Hunt were the first proprietors, followed by Charles, Emory and George W. Hunt.

"In the beginning, wet groceries [liquor] were kept as well as dry, I was told, but the C&E Hunt store was dry to my recollection. It had everything you can think of that was for sale in any country store: dry goods, hats, caps, boots, shoes, rubbers, groceries, furniture, carpets, crockery, tinware, hardware, stoves, feathers and all the other things of the day. A tailor shop and a first class tailor. Nice suitings and trimmings.

"Back of the store there was a large barn. This barn was owned by Gardner and Nicholas Hunt. In the inside it was partitioned off so each one knew just where his part was. An old eyesore in the village was the two cow yards, right beside the street. Today [1917] the barn has been torn down, the yards filled in and a nice house [10 Concord Road] has taken its place.

"I mustn't forget to tell you about the amount of business in straw braid once done at Hunt's store. People all over town and towns around, braided straw for hats. They brought it to the store and sold it according to the quality--very fine, medium or coarse--and took their pay in goods out of the store. Several times a year a team would come from the hat factories and take away quantities of the different kinds. People came 20 miles to trade their straw work for goods.

"There were the old firms of butchers, of J.D. and C.A. Cutter, also Goodnow and Rogers. The old stage line went from South Sudbury via Sudbury, Wayland and Weston to Stony Brook. Thadeus Moore, for years the owner and driver, carried the U.S. Mail, did express work, had passengers and baggage and brought us our daily paper. At the start of the [Civil] war, 26 people were on the coach besides the usual amount of baggage. It took two and a half hours to get to Boston in those days."

As Uncle Atherton turns the team east on the Post Road towards East Sudbury we pass the old shop of Edwin Arnold, the wheelwright [today's frame loft]. He tells us that there was a school over the shop for a short time and that the blacksmith shop of John P. Allen was nearby. "He and Squire Cutler and Dana Hunt always were in the old store ready to get their paper when the stage arrived," he says. "In those days, you couldn't see across the store because there was so much smoke from pipes and cigars. Not so today, nor for several years. Goods delivered after orders taken; nothing to come for often. Free delivery of all mail outside village, so nothing in that line."

We pass over Green Hill to the old Landham School House. Uncle Atherton remembers when it used to stand in the flat-iron of land at the intersection of the roads leading to Saxonville and Wayland. It has since been moved and burned and another takes its place.

"There were so many scholars that plank seats were put in the front of the first row of desks, and our feet were on the recitation platform," Uncle Atherton recalled. "The big boys would try to step on our feet so we would tuck them under our seats until class was over. Some of the boys and girls were grown up and as large as they would ever be, and there were all sizes down to five-year-old children.

"Now the school is for the first grades and only a very few scholars; but in my day, nearly 100 packed in. I'm not quite sure of the number.

"Down on the Saxonville road lived Uncle Johnny Goodnow. He wore his hair braided like a Chinaman in a pig tail down his back. He lived to be between 102 and 103 years of age. We thought him a wonder and he was to most of us young people. I can't think of one person who was at the head of a family in my boyhood days in Landham District who is alive today and so it is all over town.

"We did not have the steam or electric railways, bicycles, autos and so many ways to get around as now," Uncle Atherton muses as he turns the horses back toward home. "The beaches, mountains and places of resort were away off, in our minds, and only the few who had fine horses and carriages were able to enjoy the things that are so common today."

The sounds of war could already be heard in Sudbury, and well before the armistice was signed on November 11, 1918, the town's young men were answering the call to conflict as had every generation before them. Little did they know that this war would change Sudbury and the entire world for all time.

Atherton Rogers died on November 11, 1933, fifteen years to the day after the signing.

HELEN BLACKMER FLYNN

The Wadsworth Monument

Located on rising ground about 500 feet east of Concord Road and half a mile north of the Boston Post Road in South Sudbury, the Wadsworth Monument commemorates the Sudbury Fight on April 21, 1676 when Captain Samuel Wadsworth and 28 other soldiers lost their lives in a day-long battle with Philip of Pokonoket and more than 1,000 braves.

Dedicated in 1852 in the midst of a blinding snowstorm, the monument is designed after one at Lucca, Italy. Three blocks of granite, set one above another, form a base for a tall, tapering shaft that rises 21 1/2 feet above ground level.

Captain Wadsworth and his men were ambushed by the Indians along an old cart path in the vicinity of the present Massasoit Avenue and the battle took place to the north and east of the monument. Wadsworth and his company held their own until late in the day when the Indians set the woods on fire. The surviving soldiers retreated to the shelter of Noyes' mill in South Sudbury under the cover of darkness.

V

The Veterans Come Home

Alfred Bonazzoli remembered an eerie silence along the front-line trenches in France at the 11th hour of the 11th day of the 11th month of 1918. The word had just come down that Germany had signed the Armistice. World War I was over.

"Everyone was very solemn," he was to say later. "We just bowed our heads. We felt that we could live another day."

Time has a way of dulling memories and thinning the ranks of men that enemy shot and shell could not destroy. Only memories, fluttering flags in our cemeteries and an inscribed boulder in Grinnell Park remain today of those 32 men of Sudbury who served their country during the first great war. All but one returned to tell the tale.

Bonazzoli, whose family delivered coal to more than half the households in Sudbury, remembered the cow. His unit had found her abandoned on a French farm and brought her along to the front where she provided fresh milk until she finally became a shell casualty.

Albert Germomprez of East Sudbury remembered the silence too. He was an interpreter in company headquarters for the 3rd Battalion of the 55th Artillery Regiment when rumors of an Armistice began circulating at 9 a.m. The big guns kept firing until three minutes of eleven and suddenly all went silent. There was no cheering. Men simply stood around and looked at one another. It was not until later that evening that reality sank in and celebrations sprang up along the lines.

Alan F. Flynn, who would start a 33-year tenure in the Sudbury School System as a teacher, principal and counselor in 1927, heard the news from a hospital bed in Paris where he was recovering from the effects of German gassing and a bout with influenza. There he observed men who previously hadn't been able to sit up dancing on their beds.

Flynn's unit, the 101st Field Artillery Battery of the 26th Infantry Division, played a key role in the defense of Paris earlier that summer. On July 4, 1918, the Battery was looking forward to a well-earned leave following a parade when word came that a German advance column was eight miles from the city. The 101st quickly mobilized and was soon in position to force the Germans to begin their long and arduous retreat through Chateau Thierry.

Charlie Goodnow Jr. was another who would hear of the Armistice from a hospital bed in France. He was recovering from what he considered "slight" wounds to the ear and leg sustained in action against the Germans in Belleau Wood and St. Michiel with the Sixth Massachusetts Infantry. Harold Chandler Butterfield also served in the Sixth, seeing action in St. Nazaire and Nantes.

Others who went overseas included John T. Hutchby, an ambulance driver in France, and Fred Stone, a musician who would later assemble a popular marching band that would be a fixture for years at Sudbury Memorial Day exercises. Roland "Pete" Eaton, a machinist at Hurlbut and Rogers, and William Hellman arrived in Europe in the late stages of the war.

Eaton's 35th Engineers was the first company to enter Germany and was given the assignment of preparing bridgeheads over the Rhine for the allied occupation forces. Hellman's ship was a member of the "Suicide Fleet" which was given the job of clearing more than 48,000 German magnetic mines from the waters of the North Sea.

Sherrold Garfield enlisted in the Navy in 1917 and wound up as a Machinist Mate First Class on an 0-Class submarine. Ironically, most of his action came against friendly forces. On one occasion, his sub was attacked by a British freighter while transferring supplies at sea from a Swedish sailing ship doing tender duty, and later it was accidentally rammed by an American warship in Boston Harbor.

Many Sudbury men never left the country, but served nevertheless. Steven M.W. Gray saw action at the Chatham Naval Air Station on Cape Cod when a German U-Boat torpedoed and shelled a coal barge off Nauset Beach. Clarence "Kye" Baldwin, whose powder blue Model A Ford school bus was a fixture in North Sudbury for years, served with the Coast Artillery at Fort McKinley in Portland, Maine, and was ready to board the troopship for overseas duty when the Armistice came.

Forrest D. Bradshaw, who would later serve the town in a number of capacities, including postmaster, was another who never left these shores. Bradshaw enlisted on August 24, 1917 and spent his enlistment training observers for the Balloon Corps at Camp Morrison near Alexandria, Virginia, and later at Fort Knox in Kentucky.

Sudbury's only casualty spent less than a month in the service and never left American soil. William H. Styles, 21, enlisted on September 3, 1918 and reported for basic training at Camp Devens in Ayer. Less than two weeks later, he died of pneumonia.

American Legion Post 191 was organized two years after the Armistice, and shortly thereafter was voted the free use of the Wadsworth School, located where the police station now stands, for a meeting hall providing: "that the Legion be held responsible for the condition of building and grounds and that they shall stand the expense of such minor repairs that may be ordered by a committee composed of one member of the selectmen, one member of the Legion and one member to be chosen by the two."

Bonazzoli, Bradshaw and several other veterans of the Great War would join forces for one more mission some seven years after the Armistice. The Legion Post had renovated the old Wadsworth School and installed a pool table. Now the Legionnaires were looking for a cannon to decorate the front lawn.

They put in a request with Colonel Chase, the commanding officer of the Framingham Arsenal. The request was granted and Bonazzoli, along with Bradshaw, Albert Tallant and Major Albert Owen, a surgeon with the Old 26th "Yankee" Division, drove over in a Bonazzoli coal truck to collect it.

Chase had jurisdiction over several obsolete American field pieces as well as a huge Italian cannon that had been shipped to the United States as a prize of war. It had been firing at Americans near Les Eparges, France, on the morning of September 13, 1918, before units from the Yankee Division stormed it, taking many prisoners in the process.

The Sudbury contingent was told it could take any of the American 75-millimeter guns on the field, but not the Italian gun, which, Chase said, had been promised to another town.

But Bonazzoli had other ideas. The gun, after all, had been captured by his regiment. He and his crew quickly hitched the tongue to the tow bar of his truck and off they went to Sudbury with the cannon bouncing merrily behind.

There was an official uproar of course, but Sudbury had the cannon in a place of honor in front of the Legion Hall, and possession, after all, was nine tenths of the law. The other town settled for another German gun and that was that.

The cannon stayed in front of the Legion Hall until shortly before the building was torn down and replaced by the Police Station. It was then towed to the Highway Department on Old Lancaster Road. In 1996 it was removed to John Bartlett's greenhouses and restored. It now reposes on a permanent base on the lawn of the American Legion Post 191 Headquarters on the Boston Post Road.

What would the Sudbury boys who signed up to serve their country find when they returned home? There were subtle changes, to be sure, but most took up where they left off. A crisis in the school department developed when the teaching staff resigned en masse just prior to the start of the 1917 school year. Superintendent Frank Benedict called for an increase in the school budget in order to attract and retain replacements. The new payroll of $5,239.49 for 23 teachers prompted the six school janitors to petition the town for larger salaries.

There were also some architectural changes. Leonard and Ruth Stevens Goulding dismantled the old Moses Brewer house in Wayland and rebuilt it on a lot on Concord Road near the Wadsworth Cemetery. Antique expert and author Wallace Nutting hailed it as a "perfect 17th Century dwelling." A committee composed of Waldo Stone, Frank F. Gerry and J. Stanley Rice was negotiating a five-year street lighting contract with the Edison Illuminating Company of Boston.

Town Meeting was busy too. For the first time ever, voters considered a line-by-line budget and established set salaries for town officials instead of paying them per diem. Under the new structure, the Chairman of the Board of Selectmen received $150, the second and third Selectmen $125, Clerk of the Board $25 and Town Treasurer $175. The Town Clerk earned $150, the Auditor $25, Town Accountant $150, Moderator $25, Chairman of the Board of Assessors $125, Second and Third Assessors $75 each, School Board Chairman $75 and other members and the School Treasurer $50.

By 1919, with most of the soldiers home from the war, Sudbury's rural atmosphere, clear lakes and streams became a magnet for residents of Boston, many of whom built or rented cottages and fishing and hunting camps. Among them was a young pitcher for the Boston Red Sox baseball team. His name was George Herman "Babe" Ruth.

Stearns' Mill

Located on Dutton Road just a few yards north of Pratt's Mill Road is the site of Stearns' Mill which, until its demise in the early '60s, was the oldest grist and sawmill in continuous operation in the United States.

It was built in the year 1677, just 39 years after the Town was settled, of hewn beams fastened with wooden trunnels. It was sheathed with birch bark. The town fathers inspected the site and subsequently granted Peter King, Thomas Read Senior, John Goodenow, John Smith and Joseph Freeman liberty to build a sawmill. As part of the bargain, the town gave them 20 tons of timber from the common lands for its construction along with sufficient earth for the dam.

But there was a catch. The Grantees had to agree that "... whenever they and any of them, their heirs, executors, administrators, assigns or successors, shall either throw up their said corn mill or fail to grind the town's corn and grain and logs in season as above said, the Town's land hereby granted shall be forfeited and returned to the Town's use again."

During the Revolution, the mill ground tons of saltpeter to be made into gunpowder for the Continental Army. In Civil War days it turned out powder kegs for the Union Army and in the '50s, under the supervision of William A. Stearns, it turned out ammunition boxes for the Korean War along with wooden toys and lobster crates. (Illustration by Loring Coleman)

VI

Babe Ruth: Gentleman Farmer

Mr. and Mrs. Allen of Cambridge faced a dilemma. They had lingered over lunch and drinks during a beautiful early summer afternoon at the Wayside Inn, and arrived back at the Wayside Inn Station of the Massachusetts Central Railway just in time to see the last train for Boston disappear around the bend.

There was nothing to do but start walking. The Allens headed back down Dutton Road, hoping that someone on the State Road (Route 20) would give them a ride to Boston.

As luck would have it, help was not long in coming. An expensive Packard touring car stopped and the well-dressed driver motioned them aboard. On the way into town, Mr. Allen was impressed with the flair with which the driver handled the automobile and inquired if he drove professionally.

"No," was the reply. "I play baseball." [1]

The identity of the mysterious stranger was revealed the following morning when the Allens recognized him in a picture in the morning paper. He was Babe Ruth, star pitcher for the Boston Red Sox.

Ruth discovered Sudbury not long after he joined the Red Sox as a hitting pitcher in the spring of 1914. Several veteran Red Sox players, including his catcher, Chet Thomas, rented or owned camps in the Pine Lakes area where they could fish, hunt and party without being disturbed. By 1919, Ruth was using a camp on Willis Lake owned by sports enthusiast Larry Joyce. He continued to come to Sudbury even after he was traded to Jacob Ruppert's New York Yankees that winter.

In 1922, Ruth purchased the Sylvester Perry Farm on Dutton Road along with a camp located on Willis Lake across from what is now the end of Harness Lane. He moved his wife, Helen, and adopted daughter, Dorothy, there soon after. He dubbed the farm "Home Plate."

Ruth took a hit when the property was assessed. Sylvester Perry was not popular in town and the assessors had taken out their frustrations on him by over-assessing his property. The over-valuation was passed on to the new owner.

Ruth's purchase of the Perry place was the direct result of a horrific 1922 season during which the Bambino's weight went up and his batting average went down in direct proportion. To quiet the often vocal New York press, he held a post-season dinner at the New York Elks Club where he told the writers he was giving up hard liquor for a year and spending the winter shoveling snow and chopping wood on his Massachusetts farm. He would then go to Hot Springs, Arkansas, for pre-season workouts so as to be ready to set a new home-run record in 1923.

Helen Ruth was a good baseball wife who put up with her husband's frequent New York parties, but some believe that she engineered the move to Sudbury as part of a reconciliation. She remembered the town fondly from the days when the Babe was a young member of the Red Sox and obviously hoped that the farm's remote location would help slow down the steady stream of writers and hangers-on that plagued him constantly in New York.

The ploy worked. While the New York press carped about Ruth spending the winter in snow and seclusion in Massachusetts, the "Bambino" took on the role of gentleman farmer, rebuilding a chicken house and ordering 1,000 hens, most of which died soon after they arrived. A horse, a cow, a yearling heifer, 90 fowls, including several turkeys, and a couple of pigs came with the property. In all, he spent roughly $26,000, about half of his 1922 salary.

Ruth resolved to chop all the wood that was burned in the furnace himself, but soon fell far short of that goal. He would haul out the axe when reporters and photographers showed up but it was generally one of the neighborhood boys who finished the job.

"I used to chop wood for him," the late Mert Haskell, who grew up on the farm next to Ruth's, told Warren Russo of the *Sudbury Town Crier*. "I'd do all the work and he'd sit there and drink beer and talk to me."

When Ruth got ready to head South for the 1923 season, he told the *Hartford* (Connecticut) *Times*, that he was a changed man, both mentally and physically:

"When I came down from frozen little Sudbury, Massachusetts, I left two things behind: the old limousine with the brass-buttoned, gold braided atmosphere it created last season and, get this, TWENTY ONE pounds of flesh [from 235 to 214]," he crowed.

"And now it seems that everybody is more interested in my stomach than my home runs. Even up there in that little Massachusetts town youngsters would ask about my weight and the day I left, the garage owner waited three hours for me to come by. When I did, he pulled out a tape measure and asked me to stand still while a wager was being decided.

"The measurement was two inches less than he had wagered, and so it cost him $20. I learned afterward that the fellow who won had visited my farm every day to see if I was actually chopping wood and working hard. I proved my reduced weight pretty well to the experts up there in Sudbury."

Try as he might to take on sophistication, Ruth continued to be a rube at heart. He drove nails and spikes into the house's plastered walls to hang up baseball souvenirs and delighted in taking advantage of any sort of bargain, even if it was something that he never would use. He never forgot his early years as an orphan and hosted two or three picnics a year for local orphanages complete with games and lots of prizes including a bat, a ball or a glove for each child.

Ruth was popular with the neighborhood boys, often joining them at Stearns' Mill near his home to tell stories and play catch. Ruth had a black farm hand/chauffeur named Baily who did most of the chores. Alvin Noyes remembered watching them getting their Model T Ford farm truck stuck up to the hubs in a wet meadow near the mill.

"Ruth got an axe from the barn and cut some brush," said Noyes. "We finally got the truck out, but he left the axe.

"George Wilson spent a lot of time at the mill. He told everybody, including Ruth, that he used to catch for the Medford Nine. He squatted down and said 'Put her there, Babe.' Babe threw it and I never saw anybody throw a ball that hard. George fell right over backwards into the brook." [2]

If the whole Sudbury venture was an attempt by Helen Ruth to live a normal life with her husband and child far from the hurly-burly of New York City, the victory was a hollow one. Ruth was a born and bred city boy and, despite his love for hunting and fishing, a city boy he would remain.

Helen Ruth was both a Catholic and a Democrat, two traits that didn't endear her to some Sudbury residents at the time. Some thought she was afraid of her husband, and Forrest Bradshaw, who ran the store where the Ruths got most of their meat, described her to Ruth biographer Marshall Smelser as "a girl that seemed to be lost." [3]

Mrs. Ruth was never seen driving the family Packard. Baily, her chauffeur, drove her wherever she needed to go and tended to most of the shopping. Ruth often bought his own meat at Bradshaw's, selecting the best cuts for himself and then ordering two or three pounds of hamburger for the rest of the family. He didn't like to wait his turn and would rush in and say he was in a hurry. Other customers generally didn't mind waiting so they could tell the folks back home that they had run into the Babe while shopping.

The Ruths became customers at Bradshaw's early in the Babe's tenure in Sudbury. Not long after he moved in, a blizzard made travel by automobile impossible and the family was marooned for several days. Finally, Ruth and Baily were forced to hitch up a borrowed one-horse pung and make a foraging expedition to South Sudbury. The *Boston Sunday Globe* of January 14, 1923, picks up the story:

THE BABE NEARLY CLEANED
OUT SOUTH SUDBURY GROCER

Special Dispatch to The Globe

SOUTH SUDBURY, Jan. 13--Babe Ruth drove up to Selectman Forrest Bradshaw's general store here this morning in a one-horse pung, jumped through a snowdrift, stomped in through the door and announced that he had got to buy some grub.

Mrs. Babe trailed behind with her shopping list.

"Care if I help myself and pile the stuff here on the counter?" asked the hulking Bambino.

"Go as far as y' like," chuckled First Sergt Charlie Spiller, commander of the Sudbury Legion post and head floor walker of Mr. Bradshaw's store.

And believe Charlie, the Babe went about as far as they ever do go. He spied a box of fancy crackers and he spied a slab of cheese. He helped himself to a jar of marmalade. He filled a basket with oranges and he found a jar of peanut butter. He nailed a package of chipped beef and he seized a slab of bacon. Meanwhile, the missus was ordering such plebeian things as potatoes, carrots and beefsteaks.

"We ran all out and I'm going to stock up before another storm comes," explained the Babe. "I'm not coming poking out by pung again."

Sleighing is too slow for the big boy. And before he got through, he had piled upon the counter a mountain of groceries that added up to nigh $25--whereupon, the heavy hitter unslung his trusty fountain pen and signed George H. Ruth to one of those fancy checks of his, adorned with the face of the home run king.

They piled the stuff into the sleigh. The Babe climbed up in the seat beside his chauffeur and they headed back for that old-fashioned farm house of his, tucked away on a back road so deep in the snow that Babe Ruth's 12-cylinder roadster is stumped at last.

One horse power gets further than any motor monster in the Sudbury drifts this winter.

Ruth later complained that Baily spent too much money for groceries and had standing orders at Bradshaw's and Hunt's that the chauffeur could not exceed a certain ceiling. He was also concerned that Baily was too attentive to Mrs. Ruth.

Ruth had a fishing shack on a small pond that was part of the "Home Plate" property where he held parties for writers, ballplayers and hangers-on. When Mrs. Ruth was around, the occasions were reasonably quiet. The camp on Willis Lake, which Ruth dubbed "Ihatetoquitit", was reserved for occasions that might cause a disturbance as it was out of earshot to all but the most sharp-eared neighbors. On one occasion, Ruth was said to have thrown an upright piano off the porch of his camp and into Willis Lake. Whether or not the instrument was ever recovered is not recorded.

Ruth sold his beloved "Home Plate" after divorcing Helen in 1926. The buyer was Herb Atkinson, founder of Sudbury Laboratories and, later, the Sudbury Foundation.

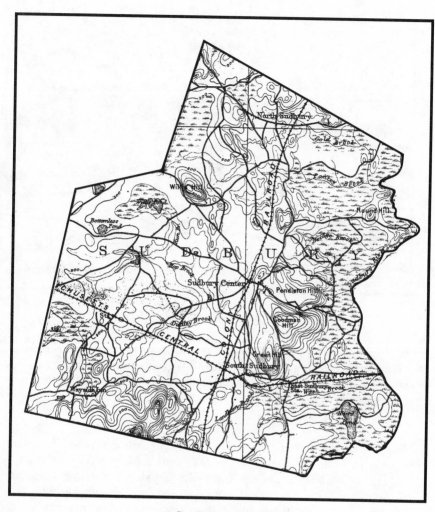

Sudbury, 1910

Longfellow's Wayside Inn

Erected as a two-room homestead in 1702 by David How and enlarged and opened as a hostelry in 1716, the Wayside Inn is Sudbury's oldest business and claims to be the oldest continuously-operating inn in the United States. It was run by four generations of the Howe family before falling into private hands.

It was during the time that the Inn was a private residence that Henry Wadsworth Longfellow visited in 1863 and subsequently used it as the setting for his book of poems, Tales of a Wayside Inn. *Later it was purchased by Edward R. Lemon, who restored it as an operating hostelry. Henry Ford bought the property from Lemon's widow and ran it until his death in 1947. Today it is operated by a public non-profit trust.*

(Illustration by Loring Coleman)

The 20's
Henry Ford, Water Rights, and The Klan

The decade of the '20s roared in on the coattails of Henry Ford's purchase of the Wayside Inn estate along with nearly 3,000 acres of land in Sudbury and surrounding towns, but the good times came to an end following the stock market crash of 1929. In between, the town struggled with rampant land speculation, bigotry and growing pains.

The decade saw outsiders try to reorganize the ancient proprietorships, which were first established upon the town's incorporation in 1639. Their aim was to acquire key water rights which would be sold to Henry Ford at a huge profit. Ford, meanwhile, was proceeding with the development of the Inn estate and the creation of the Wayside Inn Boys School. He also launched the Wash Brook Project, which aimed to turn the C.O. Parmenter mill into one of his "Village Industries." This project finally collapsed when a key landowner refused to sell his riparian rights, leaving the townspeople, especially speculators who bought up useless meadow land, at each other's throats. The decade also marked the zenith of the Ku Klux Klan in Eastern Massachusetts and the Sudbury riot of August 9, 1925, when five anti-Klansmen were shot while harassing a Klan rally on the Perley Libbey farm on the Sudbury-Saxonville line.

Sudbury, with its large Italian population, and nearby Saxonville with its Irish mill workers, were ripe targets for KKK activity. Many a white robe disguised the identity of a local merchant, upset because the primarily Roman Catholic ethnic community was taking its trade out of town.

VII

Mr. Ford Comes to Sudbury

L. Loring Brooks was beginning to feel a bit like someone who has a bull by the tail and doesn't quite dare to let go. Despite the support of some of Boston's leading citizens and even Governor Cox, his labor of love was rapidly turning from a dream into a nightmare.

Brooks, a Boston stockbroker who lived on Sunset Ridge Farm not far from the Wayside Inn, had joined Charles Francis Adams, Massachusetts House Speaker B. Loring Young, and distinguished lawyer and businessman E. Sohier Welch in forming a Wayside Inn Trust to relieve the aging Cora Lemon, widow of landlord Edward R. Lemon, of the financial and physical burdens connected with running the ancient hostelry.

An appeal went forth to philanthropists and ordinary citizens all over the northeast. Shares were priced at $100 with the Trust's declaration of purpose being: "to acquire and hold the Wayside Inn at Sudbury...so well known through the song and story of Longfellow and Hawthorne and its patronage by Washington and Lafayette and other great men of past generations." [1]

The purpose of the Wayside Inn Trust was two-fold: to preserve the Inn with its priceless antiques as nearly as possible in their original condition and, secondly, to maintain and operate the Inn as an inn.

The appeal was sent out over the names of Charles W. Eliot, Allan Forbes, Henry Cabot Lodge, Dr. Myles Standish and other notables. Its aim was to sell two thousand shares at $100 apiece and use the $200,000 raised to purchase the property from Mrs. Lemon and put it in trust for future generations of Americans to enjoy.

There was plenty of enthusiasm for the project, but little

money was forthcoming, despite glowing support from the Boston newspapers and the city's most prestigious historical organizations. Chagrined, Brooks decided to play a card of his own. He boarded a railroad car in Worcester and paid a visit on Henry Ford in Dearborn, Michigan.

Brooks' goal was to persuade Ford to purchase ten shares in the Trust, hoping that the Motor Magnate's example would attract other giants of industry to the cause. Ford was polite and listened carefully to Brooks's pitch, but remained non-committal. Brooks rode home disappointed. It appeared that his two-year quest for a new landlord at the Inn would have to continue a little longer.

As it turned out, he was wrong. Not long after the Fourth of July, Brooks received a telephone call from Dutee Flint, Ford's real estate agent in Rhode Island. Ford was interested in the Trust, Flint said, and would like to talk about it the next day, July 9, 1923 at the Copley Plaza Hotel in Boston.

Brooks hurried to the Copley bright and early the next day, but Ford was nowhere to be found. Flint was there, however, bringing with him an elaborate set of instructions which Brooks was to follow to the letter. Any kind of publicity must be avoided at all costs, Flint explained.

And so it was, on the morning of July 10, that Brooks entered the hotel from Copley Square, mingled for a time with the guests in the lobby, and exited out the west entrance to Dartmouth Street. There, as promised, was a Lincoln Zephyr limousine containing Flint and Henry Ford.

Ford signalled to chauffeur John W. Burke, who threw the Lincoln in gear and headed west by a circuitous route, just in case any members of the press were following. At Sudbury, Ford asked Brooks to show him all the property on which the trust held options, scribbling down acreages and prices as he rode.

After an extensive tour of the Inn conducted by Mrs. Cora Lemon, Brooks approached Ford once more. "Would you like to invest in ten shares?" he asked. "I'll take it all," Ford replied. [2]

And he did, and then some. Within a few days of the initial transaction with Mrs. Lemon for $60,000 for the Inn and 60 acres of land, his agents had options on 1,300 more acres, much to the consternation of local land speculators who had hoped to make a killing. By the time he was through, Ford owned nearly 2,000 acres worth some $170,855,[3] making him one of the town's leading taxpayers. His holdings included all the old Howe property and extended to the tops of Nobscot Mountain and Doeskin Hill, "to provide a fitting frame for the picture and keep hot dog stands and peanut wagons out of the front yard," as he put it.

Ford managed to get off on the wrong foot with his new Sudbury neighbors, however, holding an exclusive winter skating party and dance for business associates and Boston friends and hiring a squad of burly security men to keep party crashers and the media at arm's length. He later made it up to the town by hosting an old-timer's dancing night and inaugurating his annual Middlesex County Farmers Picnic with Harvey Firestone and Thomas Edison as honored guests.

The first five years of Ford's tenure, with one exception, were spent in refurbishing the Inn, its farms and outbuildings. Crews of laborers and stone masons began digging a new millstream and erecting the two-foot-thick stone walls for what would become the Wayside Inn Grist Mill while others shored up the Inn's foundations, and opened fireplaces that had been bricked up during Edward R. Lemon's time.

By 1925, Ford's agents had tracked down much of the original Howe family furnishings that had been scattered at the settlement of Lyman Howe's estate, and crews, under the direct supervision of Edison, were installing electric lights with bulbs shaped like candle flames. Only the Edison room, now the Drivers and Drovers room, was left with its Victorian decor and huge sleigh bed as a tribute to the great scientist.

Ford's contacts with local and state officials were sparse, but dramatic. In 1927, after discovering the Redstone Schoolhouse in nearby Sterling being used as a storage shed for the Baptist Church, he had it dismantled and rebuilt across the brook from the Inn.

Ford then approached the Sudbury School Committee, explaining that he needed a school "to accommodate the children in the families of his employees at the Wayside Inn and that he would take in some others." The Committee was reluctant at first, but approved after Ford made it clear that he would pay the teacher's salary and the costs of supplies and transportation. The school was opened on January 17, 1927 and remained so until June, 1951. [4]

In 1926, after engineers determined that heavy truck traffic on the Boston Post Road was damaging the foundations of the Inn, Ford ordered the construction of the mile-and-a-half-long Route 20 bypass. Upon its completion on December 11, 1928, he sold it to the Commonwealth of Massachusetts for $1 and never cashed the check. According to the *Boston Herald* the by-pass cost Ford $288,000.

By 1930, Ford realized he needed another school to allow the graduates from the Redstone, which taught grades one through four, to continue their education without having to be bussed to the Center School. He rebuilt the nearby Southwest District School on Peakham Road, which first opened in 1849 and later burned down. The Southwest accommodated grades five through eight. As was also the case with the Redstone, pupils at the Southwest were required to attend dancing lessons at the Inn under the direction of Dancing Master Albert "Hollywood" Haynes.

The unique Wayside Inn Boys School came into being in 1928 when 31 underprivileged boys between the ages of 16 and 18, all wards of the state who had been carefully screened for aptitude and intelligence, began to gather at the old Calvin Howe House opposite the Grist Mill dam.

Ford's stated goal was to give each boy a high school education, a salary, and the opportunity to learn a trade while working half a day on the Inn estate. The salaries were quite generous by depression standards, varying from $435 to $504 annually, depending upon age, class and ability. Out of this, each student was responsible for room and board, clothing, medical care, entertainment and laundry expenses. Each was expected to start and maintain a savings account.

The Solomon Dutton House (now 182 Dutton Road) was reno- vated to allow the expansion of the student body to 50 boys in 1931. Later the enrollment was increased again to 75. The school closed shortly after Ford's death in 1947.

Ford's talent for making lemonade out of lemons bore fruit in the form of the Martha-Mary Chapel. The 1938 Hurricane had knocked down a stand of huge white pine trees on the little knoll behind the Redstone Schoolhouse. Ford directed that the timber be cut and sawn and the lumber used to build a non- denominational chapel for the Boys School. Ground was broken in August of 1939 and the wrought iron weathervane placed on the steeple on July 30, 1940, Ford's 77th birthday.

Ford stipulated that the building, named after his and Clara Ford's mothers, Martha Ford and Mary Bryant, was to be built- -as much as possible--with materials available on the Inn prop- erty and by people who lived, worked, or attended school there. The chapel was the sixth and last Martha-Mary chapel con- structed by Ford. Four of the others are in Michigan and the fifth at Richmond Hill, Georgia.

Ford's first foray outside his Wayside Inn enclave was to create considerable consternation around the town. On June 4, 1926, the *Boston Herald* announced that Ford intended to buy the Charles O. Parmenter Grist Mill as well as all available water rights and turn the complex into one of his "village industries" in this case, to manufacture Bakelite dashboard parts.

Howard Goodnow, acting as agent for Ford, explained that obtaining water rights was crucial to the project because Ford intended to double the size of the millpond to more than 100 acres. Goodnow hastened to explain that "a great majority of the land-owners have come into line and that the land needed will become available."

Goodnow also compared the Sudbury situation to that of Flat Rock, Michigan, where Ford had dammed a small stream and put in a parts plant that employed more than 500 people at a minimum salary of $6 a day. He noted that the population of

Flat Rock was 2,000--about the size of Sudbury--and that similar prosperity could be expected here.

"In a village this size this means unheard-of wealth," he told The *Herald*. "From a sleepy country village with hardly more than one general store, it [Flat Rock] has become a town building new homes on every lot. A town with a new electric light and water system--both of them supplied, by the way, by Mr. Ford's waterpower. A town with a bank going up and another one promised...."

But there was a fly in the ointment. At least one key water rights holder, Giuseppi Cavicchio, deemed Ford's offer for a one and one half-acre chunk of meadow land between Union Avenue and the New York, New Haven and Hartford Railroad tracks, unfair and held out for an unprecedented $300,000. Cavicchio originally gave Goodnow an option to buy the property, but later changed his mind.

Cavicchio's action was not received kindly by his neighbors, many of whom stood to gain a tidy windfall from the sale of their meadowland, much of which was inaccessible for farming or haying. Ford had made it clear that his offer was an all-or-nothing proposal. If Cavicchio could not be persuaded to sell, all deals were off.

The situation was complicated somewhat on November 1, 1927, when the mill burned down, but efforts continued both before and behind the scenes to acquire Cavicchio's land and turn it over to Ford so that the project could move forward. But even discreet overtures by the selectmen were not successful. An entry in the 1939 Sudbury *Town Report* noted: "Much effort has been made by the Selectmen and other citizens of town to effect a compromise between owners of land along Wash Brook and the Ford interests so that way may be cleared for the long-awaited and much-desired establishment of a small industrial plant in Sudbury.

"Progress has been made and it is sincerely hoped that the last remaining obstacle may soon be overcome. These efforts on the part of officials have been made with the friendliest of intentions in the interests of the town only." [5]

In the end, however, efforts to sway the remaining water rights holder were to no avail and, in 1946, all parcels in the "Wash Brook Project" were sold back to their unhappy former owners.

Meanwhile, Ford had other projects in the works. On February 17, 1928, he announced acquisition of 200 acres of flat land near Mirror Lake on the Sudbury-Stow line for a possible airport and airplane parts factory. The following July he purchased the Parmenter-Garfield General Store in Sudbury Center, had it sawed in half, and moved it with teams of oxen to a new site next to the old Hager's millpond on Route 20 in Marlborough. On June 20, 1930, it opened once more as the Wayside Inn Roadside Market with Clara Ford on hand to wait on the first customers.

Henry Ford would remain a presence in Sudbury until he died in 1947, but after the town had politely rebuffed his offer of the Parmenter-Garfield store lot as a site for the new Town Hall in 1930, he confined most of his activity to the Wayside Inn Estate.

The Wayside Inn Grist Mill

When Henry Ford bought the Wayside Inn, one of his first projects was the construction of the Wayside Inn Grist Mill. He insisted that the mill operate by water power and spared no expense in obtaining authentic 18th century milling equipment. In order to meet his criteria that the mill last for 100 years, millwright John Blake Campbell of Philadelphia ordered two runs of French Burr millstones from quarries in France, designed and built the 18-foot steel water wheel and obtained the latest in milling machinery.

The mill is built of local fieldstone brought to the site from the slopes of Nobscot Mountain with oxen and a stone boat. The rafters and beams are cut from American chestnut which was killed by the chestnut blight of the early '20s.

The mill was completed in time to grind the corn meal for Mr. Ford's Thanksgiving dinner in November of 1929 and continues to grind corn meal and whole wheat flour for the Wayside Inn bakery.

(Illustration by E. Laurie Loftus)

The Old Tramp House

This building once stood on the Meachen property on Old Marlborough Road, not far from its intersection with Willis Road. The Meachen property, which passed back into the hands of the town in 1997, was once the town poor farm and provisions had to be made to house tramps and wandering vagrants.

The tramp house, torn down in the '60s, was last used in 1917. It was a one-room building with stove, rough plank table, wooden bunks and a couple of chairs. Tramps were required to report by 4 p.m. during the short winter months and 6 p.m. during the summer when days were longer. They were fed and locked in for the night and required to pay for their room and board the following day by chopping wood or performing chores around the farm.

Tramp houses came into being as a safeguard against barn fires which were often blamed on tramps sleeping and smoking in the haymows. A surprising number of tramps were fed and housed by the town each year. The 1904 Sudbury Town Report lists 192 as fed and bedded for the year at the cost of some $38.

VIII

The Klan

Chief of Police Seneca W. Hall knew it was going to be a rough night. Ku Klux Klan meetings were generally tame affairs, but this one looked to be different. Tensions between Klansmen and local Catholics--especially the Irish mill workers from Saxonville who had fallen on hard times--had been building for weeks and finally reached the point that state police motorcycle troopers had been required to prevent a riot at the Perley Libbey farm in East Sudbury just the previous week.

Chairman of the Board of Selectmen Charlie Way had called Hall the morning of August 9, 1925, and warned of trouble. He had also called the Framingham State Police barracks. Hall responded by assigning two officers and himself to the scheduled KKK meeting at the Libbey farm on Landham Road near the border with Framingham. Normally, one detail patrolman, whose main duty was to direct traffic and quell any disturbances by hecklers, was all that was necessary.

Now Hall was expecting trouble and his instincts were right. For several weeks, turmoil had been brewing in East Sudbury, and word went around town that August 9 would be no exception. Feelings were running high against the Klan, and the Klansmen had vowed to defend themselves if necessary.

After dark, groups began to assemble. The Klansmen in their great white hoods gathered in the field behind the barn at the Libbey farm. Anti-Klansmen and excitement seekers mingled on the roadside. Among the observers was young Clarence Ames who often followed his father, Oliver, to KKK rallies on his bicycle only to be sent home when his presence was discovered.

"There were between 150 and 200 of them there at the meeting," he said "They had big white hats on so nobody could tell who they were." [1]

As the crowd of observers swelled and the dirt road between

Sudbury and Saxonville became clogged with autos, the Klan leaders meeting in the Libbey house phoned for reinforcements from surrounding towns. These started to arrive after midnight, many of them swinging clubs as they drove through the rapidly-growing mob of anti-Klansmen.

The situation escalated rapidly. Sticks and stones began to fill the air and Chief Hall and his officers, realizing that there was little they could do to control such a large number of people, drew back.

Suddenly, several shots rang out from between the henhouse and the Libbey dwelling, followed in quick succession by several more. Five men fell to the street. The crowd dispersed in all directions, but not before the wounded were piled into nearby autos and driven to the office of Dr. Christopher J. Carr on Central Street in Saxonville.

Aroused from his bed, Carr applied first aid and also notified State and Framingham police that he had patients with gunshot wounds. Crowds gathered around the house and a priest was summoned to administer last rites to Alonzo Foley of Saxonville who suffered buckshot wounds to the head. Also injured were William Bradley, Central Street, Framingham, with a bullet wound in his right thigh below the hip; Frank Maguire, Water Street, Saxonville, with buckshot wounds about the body; Edmund Purcell, High Street, Framingham, buckshot wounds to the head, and Thomas Sliney, Concord Street, Framingham, who suffered superficial injuries.

Maguire, Purcell and Sliney were not injured seriously and were allowed to leave the hospital. Foley eventually recovered from his wounds.

Bradley had arrived via a side road just before the shooting started. "We were standing in the road looking for some signs of Klansmen," he told the *Middlesex News* in 1981. "And then, all of a sudden, out of the woods came 'bang!, bang!' and Lonnie Foley got hit with buckshot right in the temple and fell in the street right next to me. And Eddie Purcell got hit with a .22 shot. I saw the blood running down his face and said: 'hey! let's get out of here.'" He received buckshot wounds in the thigh while trying to drag Foley to the safety of a nearby asparagus field.

Although stones were thrown and clubs were observed, the police were unable to find anyone injured except by shot. Several autos in the roadway were damaged.

The Framingham Taxi Company Ambulance, driven by Henry C. Boyle, was on the scene in Saxonville in minutes and transported the wounded to Framingham Hospital. Boyle was accompanied by Dr. Carr, who dressed wounds and made every effort to save Foley's life.

At the Framingham police station, Lt. John J. Sheehan immediately dispatched patrolman John F. McKenna to the scene and notified Chief William W. Holbrook. McKenna found a crowd of 100 youths milling on the road. State Police details from Concord and Framingham, commanded by Lieutenant Charles T. Beaupre, arrived at about the same time and rode their motorcycles into the crowd to restore order. Beaupre immediately radioed for reinforcements from Holden and Reading.

The forty-five men remaining in the Libbey field were marched into the house by state police, identified, transferred to two state trucks, and driven to the Framingham police station on South Street. By the time they arrived, a large and angry crowd was waiting. Chief Holbrook called all Framingham officers to emergency duty and cleared the streets.

Information that one of the victims wasn't expected to live caused the state police to take immediate action. Beaupre ordered that all men present on the estate and those attending the meeting be held on a charge of being suspicious persons where a felony has been committed.

A subsequent police search found 20 more men hiding in the barn. These were rounded up and held in a field while the police searched for weapons. Eight more youths, including Leroy Hall, 23-year-old son of the Chief, were found hiding in the bushes some distance from the rear of the barn.

State troopers found two shotguns, one rifle, a revolver, several belts of ammunition and several handsful of bullets. One rifle was found in the back seat of a Ford touring car with the chamber loaded and clogged. A handful of loaded shells were found in the car. Clubs, stones and other missiles were found strewn along the ground.

At the Framingham station, Capt. George Parker, commander of the state police patrol, assistant District Attorney Warren E. Bishop of Wayland and Detective Edward J. Sherlock, took over the investigation. Questioning continued throughout the night and the list of suspects was reduced from 75 to 24. All were scheduled to appear before Judge G. W. Blodgett the following morning.

Those charged and required to provide $200 surety included Perley W. Libbey, Robert Atkinson, Ralph Chamberlain, Oliver E. Ames and Harry Rice of Sudbury; Robert E. Diamond of N. Easton; Andrew Tervo, Calvin Whitney and Mattie Sironen of Maynard; Stanley Stevenson of Stow; Everett Brown, James R. Knowles, Warren M. Parker and Ralph E. Ambrose of Needham; Fred W. Hough of Wellesley; Herbert Nelson of Newton; James Burghart of Waltham; James Banes, Hal Buck, Russell Burks and Edmond J. Purcell of Framingham; Winfred E. LaMarine and Dennis McSweeny of Wayland along with Francis J. Maguire and Thomas P. Sliney of Saxonville. The charges against Burk, Purcell, Maguire, Sliney, McSweeny, Buck, Banes, LaMarine and Ames were later dismissed. [2]

"That trouble was expected now comes to light," *The Framingham News* reported in retrospect. "Several KKK meetings have been held in Sudbury the past few weeks and a week ago, a crowd of curious gathered on the street adjacent to the meeting. At that point it was reported that only the presence of state police prevented a disturbance.

"Since then there has been talk of trouble at this week's meeting. Alleged Klan members gathered to protect the Libbey property from damage. They gathered with the arms that were found by the police and prepared to answer any attack."

Klan membership had peaked in Sudbury in the early '20s as the older Yankee and Scandinavian residents became alarmed at the influx of Southern and Central Europeans and Irish into Sudbury and surrounding communities. They distrusted the Jews and the Catholic Church and fretted that the numerous Italian families who bought cheap farmland in South and East Sudbury would proliferate and take control of the town. The Pope, some said, would soon be calling the shots in America.

The KKK's rolls in Sudbury in the early '20s included some of the town's leading merchants, farmers, and citizens. Some joined to protect the 19th Century way of life in Sudbury while others were attracted by the KKK's strong stand on Prohibition and the separation of church and state. Still others objected that the Italians and Irish traded out of town and did not patronize local stores and services.

1924 and '25 had seen a great deal of Klan activity in East Sudbury. Meetings were held at Libbey's and in a tent on the farm of Elmer and Henry Smith on Woodside Road. Temporary policeman Howard Burr billed the town for attending eight Klan meetings between August 8 and September 24, 1924, and the summer of 1925 was just about as busy. [3]

But there were signs that the popularity of the hooded knights was waning both nationally and locally. Catholics, Jews and anti-prohibitionists not only began boycotting businesses owned or run by suspected Klansmen, but often challenged them at their rallies. Such was the case at the Libbey farm where, earlier that year, a motorcycle squad of State Troopers had to be called to disperse a crowd and prevent a potential riot. It was shortly after this that the Klansmen vowed to arm themselves and shoot in self-defense if necessary.

This had almost happened a week before at Westwood where both Libbey and Leroy Hall were arrested and charged with carrying weapons without a license. Each was sentenced to a year in jail on August 12, 1925, but neither served any time.

The News reported on August 20, 1925, that charges against 16 defendants including Sudbury's Libbey, Atkinson, Chamberlain and Rice, were dismissed because the prosecution was unable to proceed. The State told the Court that evidence supporting charges of assault with a dangerous weapon would be presented to a grand jury later if appropriate.

Under questioning by Judge Edward W. Blodgett, the Klansmen said they were tired of being beaten up and injured by anti-Klansmen, so this time they had decided to arm themselves. They insisted that they had fired only after having been attacked.

Before making his ruling, Judge Blodgett made it clear to the Klansmen that, while they had the right to assemble under the Constitution, they did not have the right to assemble under arms. "If a shooting occurs and the one who shoots is apprehended, he is responsible," he warned the defendants. "The fact that you were attacked with stones does not give you the license to use firearms." [4]

The Libbey Farm Riot proved to be the high water mark of the Ku Klux Klan both in Sudbury and Eastern Massachusetts. Officials and police hounded suspected Klansmen to the point where the ceremonial robes and hoods that once were worn proudly at cross burnings and rallies were hidden away in trunks in attics and garrets. Klansmen who owned businesses in town kept their heads down for fear of boycotts by Catholics.

Although some hate and bigotry against foreigners, Catholics and Jews remained well into the '50s and '60s, the fiery cross of the Knights of the Ku Klux Klan sputtered out within the boundaries of Sudbury, hopefully never to be seen again.

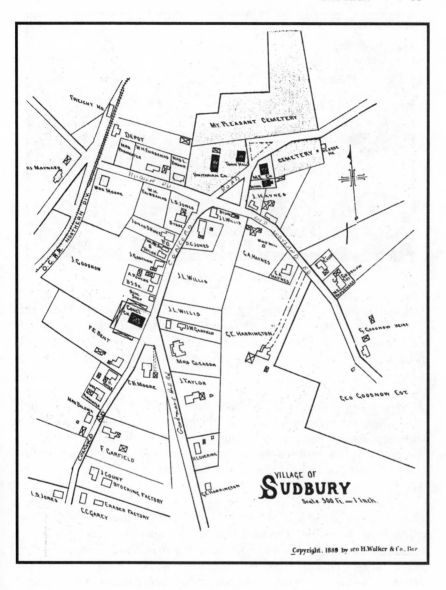

VILLAGE OF
SUDBURY
Scale 500 Ft. = 1 Inch.

THE OLD GOULDING HOUSE

The Old Goulding House

Originally built in Wayland by the heirs of Jonathan Maynard, this 17th Century house was purchased by antique dealer Leonard P. Goulding in 1918, taken apart beam by beam, and reconstructed faithfully on the east side of Concord Road just north of the Wadsworth Cemetery.

Mr. Goulding, a practicing antique dealer and an authority on early New England antiquities, restored the house with a view to making it a showplace for his fine collection of antiques. When the work was complete, it was restored exactly to the smallest detail of how it first appeared on land granted to Jonathan Maynard between 1690 and 1700.

With its small-pane leaded windows and salt box design, the building attracts considerable attention. Within, the house is equally charming with a huge central chimney dividing the first floor rooms. The fireplaces are huge and designed for cooking. The support beams are exposed, the walls paneled and a secret hideout stands ready to protect the family in case of Indian attack.

(Illustration by Dorothy Linscott Clarke)

IX

Sudbury Proprietee Reorganized

Henry Ford's announcement in the June 6, 1926, edition of the *Boston Herald* that he planned to buy the C.O. Parmenter Mill in South Sudbury and establish one of his famous "village industries" drew more than casual interest from at least one Sudbury resident. A short time after the news hit the streets, Earl J. Boyer, innkeeper at the Wayside Inn, received a visit from one Warren Wetherbee to discuss a "certain proposition."

"I stopped the conversation then and there," Boyer later told the *Boston Transcript*. "I told him that no matter what his proposition was, it would not interest me." [1]

Had Boyer and the good citizens of Sudbury realized at that time just what Wetherbee had in mind, the chances are that they would have been very interested in his proposition, albeit probably for the wrong reasons. Wetherbee, his father, H.J. Wetherbee, and Samuel D. and Edward J. Hannah of Bourne, indeed had a plan. They were going to revive the ancient Proprietee that was formed when Sudbury was founded, take title to any unclaimed land and water rights, clear title to these rights and sell them to Henry Ford at a handsome profit.

In 17th Century New England, the Proprietors were the original grantees or purchasers of a tract of land, usually a township, that they and their heirs, assigns or successors, together with those they saw fit to admit to their number, held in common ownership. They enjoyed the absolute ownership and exclusive control of such tracts of land as were granted to them.[2] Wetherbee and the Hannahs were convinced that they held the power as Proprietors to settle the disposition of any unclaimed lands, specifically, the water rights on Hop Brook which Giuseppi Cavicchio refused to sell to Ford.

They hatched their plot on February 4, 1928. Warren E. Wetherbee and Samuel D. Hannah contacted Chief of Police and Constable Seneca Hall to witness postings of warrants of a Proprietors' meeting on bulletin boards at the Old Town Hall and Memorial Congregational Church.

The Warrant:

A meeting of proprietors of Sudbury Plantation will be held February seventh, 1928, at 8 O'Clock p.m. at the home of H.J. Wetherbee, Concord Road, Sudbury, Mass to vote the following articles:

Art. 1st--Election of officers

Art. 2nd--Method of calling future meetings

Art. 3rd--To raise money to conduct the Proprietors' affairs and business

Art. 4th--To determine whether the clerk elected at the meeting shall be given authority to make a search of the records and determine if the Sudbury Plantation and the said Proprietors own any land, waters and rights which may be sold, and if any land, waters and rights etc. are found, what disposition shall be made of them.

Art. 5th--To determine whether the clerk elected is to receive any expense for the purpose of conducting the affairs of the proprietors.

Art. 6th--To determine what action will be taken as to lands, waters, rights etc. originally owned by the Proprietors, but which were divided and later abandoned.

Art. 7th--To determine whether the clerk elected is to be given authority to make deeds or releases of lands, waters, rights etc. which he may sell or otherwise dispose of.

Art. 8th--To act upon any other business presented at the meeting.

WARREN E. WETHERBEE
A proprietor of the Sudbury Plantation [3]

Wetherbee asked Chief Hall for an affidavit certifying that he had witnessed the posting. Hall gave him one, but, because he was ill, never actually saw the notices being tacked to the bulletin boards. He later returned to check both boards and discovered that the warrants were missing. The following morning, Forrest Bradshaw found one copy hidden beneath the Town Hall steps with no tack holes in it. Bradshaw ran off several hundred copies on his mimeograph machine and they were soon distributed all over town.

Hall immediately sent special police officer Fred Elser to fetch Wetherbee, who was attending an American Legion meeting at the old Wadsworth Schoolhouse. Wetherbee reposted the notices, but later testified that both were missing the following morning.

It was obvious that Wetherbee and Hannah had hoped that no one would see the warrants and that the only people attending the meeting at Wetherbee's house on Concord Road would be the Hannah and Wetherbee families. Unfortunately for them, this was not to be the case. The evening of February 5, more than 40 citizens--all concerned that they might find their titles clouded--met at Bradshaw's and hired lawyers A. Van Allen Thompson and Harold Williams to represent their interests.

Thompson and Williams recommended Quo Warranto court action that would thwart the proposed attempt of the Wetherbees and Hannahs to do in Sudbury what they were already trying to do on Cape Cod--revive the ancient proprietee which held title to certain lands and rights on Nobscot Mountain, the Sudbury River meadows and local rivers and streams.

The Wetherbees and Hannahs were already involved in litigation under consideration by Judge Wait of the Massachusetts Supreme Judicial Court to determine by what right Hannah revived the Cape Cod proprietees. There was also a case before Judge Davis of the land court, where Raymond M. Adams of Brookline sought to have title registered in his name to a piece of property claimed by Mrs. Wetherbee to have been obtained by her from the Cape Cod Proprietee.

Boyer later told The *Boston Transcript* that Wetherbee approached him about adjusting Ford Titles to Wayside Inn property. Boyer declined the offer, noting that all Ford's titles were insured.

At 8 p.m. February 7, the time set for the meeting, a delegation of about 150 men and women formed a caravan at the town hall and drove to the nearby Wetherbee house on Concord Road. Besides 50 actual descendants of proprietors, there were about 100 "sightseers."

Everyone who so desired was given entrance to the house, with Chief Hall on hand to keep order. In the living room they found Warren Wetherbee, Samuel D. Hannah and his son Edwin J. Hannah. There was a prolonged and awkward silence before Wetherbee opened the meeting.

Attorney Thompson rose to question the legality of the meeting, but Hannah and Wetherbee insisted they were in the right and invited anyone wishing to participate in the meeting to step forward and prove they were descended from one of the original Proprietors. About 40 men and women stepped forward, gave their names and addresses and said that they would provide proof of ancestry "when the time came." As far as they were concerned, they were just as much Proprietors as Wetherbee and Hannah.

After an hour of collecting names and addresses, Wetherbee reopened the meeting, only to have someone nominate Bradshaw as moderator. Not being a descendant of a proprietor, Bradshaw wasn't eligible, but Harvey N. Fairbank, Chairman of the Board of Selectmen, was quickly nominated and elected. Reverend Elbridge C. Whiting was elected clerk and immediately someone moved to reconvene the meeting at the Town Hall where there was more room.

At the Town Hall, Fairbank dispensed with the remainder of the agenda and asked Thompson to explain what was going on. Thompson told the people gathered, most of whom were concerned that they might not hold clear title to their lands, that the continued existence of the Proprietee was questionable at best, as was the possibility of it being revived.

Hannah countered that there was no question that the meeting was properly called by the proper persons and that the Proprietee definitely did exist. He also assured the crowd that no individual's title would be endangered.

Someone asked why then did Hannah want to revive the Proprietee, and Wetherbee responded that the only question concerned some wild lands which could be clearly settled as to ownership in no other way--only meadow land and some on Nobscot Mountain, he said. No one need be concerned about his titles. "Why the fuss over waste land?" someone said. "I think someone wants to claim it," countered Fairbank to a series of snickers.

Wetherbee elaborated that the lands in question were along the Sudbury River, the marshes, some of the streams and on Nobscot Mountain. They could all be disposed of in one evening, he said.

Former Assessor Fred Ham questioned this assertion, noting that he knew of no unclaimed lands in Sudbury. Ernest Little moved that the chairman appoint a committee of five to investigate titles, legalities etc. and report to a legally called meeting in the near future.

Hannah later told reporters he planned to wait until the body abolished itself, but since he had lost control of the proprietorship he was unsure as to what he could do. He told the *Boston Transcript* that the whole idea of reviving the proprietorship was not his or Wetherbee's at all, but was broached by those desirous of selling water rights to Ford. It was planned to revive these proprietary rights, establish a clear title and then sell at a high rate to Ford. This idea, he said, was fostered by certain residents of the town who, the previous night, appeared in opposition and took the meeting from the hands of Wetherbee.

Hannah explained that if Ford held the proprietor's rights, he could petition to register the whole area that he wants to improve (including the Giuseppi Cavicchio plot). His claim would then go to Land Court where his rights would be recognized and the whole situation in the swamplands in Sudbury Basin would be cleared up.

Hannah claimed that his chief adversary to a satisfactory settlement was the Ku Klux Klan, which was known to be especially strong in Sudbury. He charged that the majority of the

townspeople at the meeting were Klan members or sympathiz-
ers and that the Klan's "riot squad" and signal men were in
attendance. Had not the meeting gone supposedly in the townspeople's favor, violence might have resulted, he said.

Bradshaw, one of the prime movers against Warren Wetherbee,
denied that the Ku Klux Klan had taken any hand in the matter. The Klan, he said, had not been active for four years in
Sudbury and any charges that it had participated in the present situation were false and ridiculous. (He neglected to mention that Klansmen and Saxonville Irish bricklayers and mill
workers rioted August 9, 1925, just three years earlier, at the
Libby Farm on the Sudbury-Framingham line.)

"For ten days I have been investigating these rights, visiting
courts and libraries in Boston and talking with lawyers,"
Bradshaw told *The Transcript*. "I have found that, with the
exception of certain lawyers and judges who have worked on
the Cape Cod case, no one in the entire state understands the
ancient proprietees except Mr. Hannah and his associates.

"The charges then, that they did [understand the proprietee]
and that they [the proprietees] were to have been revived by
residents of this town in order to extract large sums from
Henry Ford as stated in your [*Boston Transcript*] interview
with Mr. Hannah are not only false, but they are comic. I deny
them on my own behalf as well as one of the citizens who will
seek Quo Warranto proceedings against Wetherbee on behalf of
the other citizens of this town.

"The thorough silliness of the Klan charges to anyone who
knows anything about the Klan in this region are so ridiculous
that they answer themselves. They exist only in the imagina-
tion of Mr. Hannah."

The principals had their day in court before Judge Wait on
February 10, 1928. Judge Wait denied petition for Quo
Warranto by five citizens of Sudbury including Forrest
Bradshaw, against Warren Wetherbee, Samuel Hannah and
others.

Judge Wait was prepared to take the matter under advisement

and settle once and for all whether there is any precedent to allow the reorganization of the ancient proprieties. But he changed his mind and dismissed the case when both lawyers pointed out that the original petitioners (the Hannahs and Wetherbees) no longer controlled the proprietee.

Fairbank named a committee of five to inquire whether there were any lands or rights to which the proprietors might have title, and, if so, report back to the proprietors to have them determine what was to be done. The committee consisted of Bradshaw, Fred R. Stone, Percival W. Jones, H.H. Rogers and Ernest L. Little.

Fairbank also directed that any unclaimed lands be deeded to the town by the Sudbury Plantation, which would then dissolve itself forever.

On March 25, 1929, The Town Meeting had the final say on the matter, voting that: "The Town assume the responsibility of accepting from the heirs of the original proprietors of the Sudbury Plantation all claims, rights, titles and interests of any and all nature without redress which may have been held originally by the Proprietors and to handle as seems fair to all persons concerned, any claims to said lands, water rights or buildings situated now or formerly in the original town of Sudbury with its additional grants." [4]

While their claims to Cape Cod lands were denied by Judge Waite in the Yarmouth Case, the Hannahs and Wetherbees did gain a significant victory that would come back to roost in Sudbury some 40 years later. Judge Waite ruled that it was legal to reorganize an ancient proprietee if land was found which had escaped division through error.

The Sudbury case involved the old training field on Old County Road in East Sudbury. For some years, the ownership of this piece of property where militia and minute companies had drilled since the early 18th Century had been questioned, with various individuals laying claim to it. The matter came to a head in 1968 and the Selectmen authorized Bradshaw to attempt to establish the present legal owners.

Bradshaw discovered that the training field was one of three laid out by the Proprietors "for a perpetual Comon for training fields," and could find no records of any sales to private individuals until the Proprietee disbanded around 1805. There were records of two attempts to sell portions of the training field in 1774, but both were turned down by Town Meeting.

On April 2, 1792, The Town, evidently in a move to challenge the authority of the Proprietors, sold the field to Ephraim Carter and demanded that the Proprietors deliver all plans and records of undivided land to the Town Clerk. The Proprietors, declaring they had control of all undivided lands, refused to do so. The sale never was consummated.

Bradshaw concluded that the training field and several other small properties in town, notably the site of the Landham School House at the corner of Landham Road and the Boston Post Road, were part of the undivided land and should be dealt with under the action authorized by Article 33 of the Town Meeting of 1929.

The Town concurred with with Bradshaw's recommendation, negotiating a settlement with the Philbob Real Estate Trust which returned the training field to The Town.

Henry Ford's Wash Brook Project never materialized and eventually all his land purchases were sold back to their original owners. Sudbury would not become the Utopia that Ford and some people envisioned and, as far as the majority of the townsfolk were concerned, it was just as well.*

* Just what the Hannahs and the Wetherbees were trying to accomplish--aside from lining their pockets--is a matter of conjecture. They may have been acting as agents for other landowners/speculators looking for a windfall at Ford's expense, or they may have been simply seeking a way by which the Cavicchio land could be secured so that the project could go forward. Ford's secrecy in his early dealings for the Wayside Inn properties drew criticism from local landowners hoping to make a killing on land that was marginal at best. Cavicchio's refusal to sell his water rights to Ford left at least one prominent citizen of the town holding title to worthless meadowlands bought on speculation.

That notwithstanding, there was no question that the town could use extra revenue. At a Special Town Meeting on May 11, 1925, a proposal to build a new Center School to accommodate the upper grades and provide space for physical education, assembly halls and offices, was first approved in principle and then defeated. The Finance Committee recommended against $2,500 for planning the $75,000 project. A year later a proposal for $50,350 for alterations and an addition to the present Center School was passed.

It was obvious that more schoolrooms were needed. Enrollment had slowly crept up to 210 (46 in high school) in 1926, requiring 12 teachers and helping push the tax rate to $31 per thousand.

Earlier, the town voted to accept a gift of $3,000 from Lydia Raymond in honor of her late husband to be called the George J. Raymond Scholarship Fund for the promotion of higher education at the Sudbury High School.

Raymond, who started a lucrative dry goods business selling hats from a pushcart in Boston, first bought the old Hunt farm on what was to become Raymond Road as a summer retreat. Later he and his wife retired there. They are buried in the family mausoleum just off Warren Road.

The New Town Hall

When the old Town Hall burned on the afternoon of February 5, 1930, plans were immediately made to build a new and more roomy structure as soon as possible. Charles H. "Charlie" Way, a Sudbury man, was hired as architect and came up with a Greek-Doric design that featured the familiar four white pillars that support the lofty roof of the portico.

Thanks to the dedication of a building committee chaired by Harvey Fairbank and including Harland H. Rogers, A.M. Beckwith, Henry E. Rice, Col. Thomas S. Bradlee, Mrs. Lydia G. Raymond, Frank F. Gerry, clerk; Ralph Barton and Mrs. Melvin Guptill, two of the old Haynes barns were moved and the new hall finished in early 1932, almost two years to the day from the time the old one burned. It was dedicated with appropriate ceremony on Washington's Birthday, February 22, 1932.

Aside from the substitution of red brick and other fire-resistant materials, the new hall is in actuality an enlarged version of the old one. Historian Leslie Hall called it "an attempt to retain the charm of the old meeting house." Everyone who drives by agrees that the builders succeeded.

The '30s

Conflagration, Murder, Tempest and Celebration

To the casual observer, Sudbury was still a quiet country town in 1930, but there were rumblings beneath the surface. Henry Ford continued to develop his Wayside Inn property, which helped provide work for local laborers idled by the Great Depression, but was losing interest in his Wash Brook Project, which would have turned the C.O. Parmenter mill into a small factory manufacturing parts for Ford cars.

Ford finished the Wayside Inn Grist Mill project in 1929 and miller Erwin Smith of Hopkinton ground the first meal between the huge French Burr millstones on Thanksgiving morning of that year. That same winter, Ford purchased the William W. Parmenter General Store in Sudbury Center, sawed it in half, placed it on runners and hauled it across town to a new site next to Hager's pond in Marlborough where it became the Wayside Country Store for all time. The following year, Parmenter announced plans to operate a small general store in an addition to his house.

Town Meeting of 1929 officially put an end to the proprietorship controversy by voting the town as the official repository for all claims, rights, titles and interests of any and all nature, without redress.

Meanwhile, interests were turning in other directions. The town's first housing development, King Philip Heights, was laid out and offered "Moderately priced, generous plots of land." The old Town Hall burned to the ground, a skeleton was discovered by workmen excavating a cellar on Water Row and the 1938 Hurricane stripped the town bare of much of its standing timber.

The School Committee came under fire in 1937 when it expelled five Jehovah's Witness children for refusing to salute the flag. Jacob F. Rand, father of two of the children, declared the move unconstitutional and said that the children would be tutored at home. He noted that the conduct of the children was exemplary in every other way, and compared the ruling to Hitler's regime in the days leading up to World War II.

The region was in the depths of the Great Depression, and things looked as if they would get worse before they got better. President Franklin Delano Roosevelt's New Deal was welcomed in Sudbury in 1933 with a two-page tribute in the *Town Report* from the Selectmen who admitted, hide-bound Republicans though they were, that: "Whatever our political affiliations, we must admit that the situation has changed. The average American citizen has been able to throw off that feeling of hopelessness and despair of ever getting out of the rut and has kindled within him that spark of hope so essentially necessary to his kindling an orderly fight back to better times."

The Selectmen also warned that, as of January 1, 1934, there were more than $40,000 of uncollected taxes on the books, "the largest, in the Town's history, for this time of year."

The decade ended on a high note with a gala Tercentenary celebration.

X

Conflagration

A terse entry in Chief Seneca W. Hall's police log for February 5, 1930, served notice as to what kind of decade the '30s were going to be.

"3:15 p.m. The Town Hall was burned to the ground."

The old wooden building, which had stood on land owned by the Unitarian Church since 1846, was quickly consumed by flames fanned by a brisk wind. The fire was discovered by several members of the Sudbury Women's Club, including Mildred Davis Tallant, who were preparing for their monthly meeting.

"Mrs. Rogers was smoking in the dressing room when Esther Ellms came to the door and said 'I think the hall is on fire.'" Mrs. Tallant recalled. "My sister, Ruth Eaton, was going to play the violin. She rushed up to the stairs to get it and just then the curtain came down in a sheet of flames." [1]

Firemen from Sudbury, Marlborough, Wayland and Longfellow's Wayside Inn poured water on the flames and selectmen Harvey Fairbank and Aubrey Borden dashed into the smoke-filled building, snatched record books and relics and tossed them out an open window. Among the items saved were a colonial voting machine more than a century old and the town jury box from which the names of jurors to the Cambridge Court were drawn.

The fire evidently started in a defective chimney and efforts to extinguish it were hampered by sub-zero temperatures that froze water in the hose lines. For a time, it appeared that the Methodist and Unitarian churches nearby would be threatened. The loss was estimated at $75,000, only $7,000 of which was covered by insurance. Unlike the building that would soon replace it, the old town hall was made entirely of wood.

Town Clerk Frank F. Gerry, who was in Boston at the time of the fire, was correct in his prediction that the town vault would protect the ancient town records from the heat and flames, but Chief Hall had to guard them for two days and nights before the vault was cool enough to open safely.

One good thing was to come out of the fire. A little more than a year later, Sudbury appointed William "Ethan" Davison as the first chief of its full-fledged fire department, complete with two new trucks and a fire station under the new Town Hall. He commanded two officers, eighteen privates and four substitutes, but only one, Leo Quinn, was full-time. In addition to his fire-fighting duties, Quinn was the Town Hall janitor.

The fire left the town without a place to hold the annual March Town Meeting. The old Parmenter Store building, where once town meetings were convened on the second floor, had been purchased by Henry Ford and moved to the shores of Hager's Pond in Marlborough, not too far from the Wayside Inn. The meeting was eventually held at the High School.

One of the first actions of that meeting was to appoint a committee to "consider the matter of location, design, and cost of a municipal building." The committee was chaired by Selectman Harvey Fairbank and included Lydia G. Raymond, Temperance Oakes Guptill, Albert M. Beckwith, Henry E. Rice, Town Clerk Frank F. Gerry, Harland H. Rogers, Ralph H. Barton and Thomas Stevenson Bradlee, all distinguished citizens of the community.

After considering four possibilities, including the site of the old town hall and the lot recently vacated by the Parmenter General Store, the committee settled on a site across the road from the old hall which was then occupied by Joel Haynes' barn. Haynes occupied the 12-acre farm which once had belonged to the Rev. Israel Loring, Sudbury's first minister west of the river.

The town was able to secure the Haynes farm and buildings for $15,000, roughly the same amount of money that it would have cost to grade the alternate sites sufficiently to accommodate a building. Local architects Charles Way, Ralph Adams Cram and Joseph E. Chandler estimated that the building itself could be constructed for $65,000, increasing the entire cost of the project to $80,000.

The Committee's goal was to propose a building that retained the charm of the old hall but with the conveniences and facilities that would serve the town well in the 20th Century and beyond: "That in design it be as near a reproduction of the old hall as is practicable and becoming; that the building provide an upper hall seating capacity of 500, together with a stage, offices for town officers, suitable vaults, fire engine room, a branch library room, a banquet hall to seat 260 people, adaptable to certain school activities not provided in their present building..." [2]

The specifications called for dark red brick construction with the exception of the portico, front wall, cornices and gables which would be of wood painted white. Two vaults would be constructed to store town records and there would be space in the basement for three fire engines. The Loring Parsonage would be retained as a residence for the town hall janitor or a permanent call firefighter and the Haynes barn would be dismantled and rebuilt for the use of the town highway department on a remote corner of the property near the town pound. Way was commissioned to draw up plans and supervise the work. Perkins and Wells of Concord were the contractors.

The Committee, architect and builders did their job swiftly and well. On February 22, 1932, before a crowd that included nearly every resident of Sudbury and many former residents as well, Way turned over the keys to the new hall to Building Committee Chairman Fairbank as the 15 oldest residents looked on.

At the close of the exercises, a memorial box was placed in a stone outside the entrance to the building. The box contained the minutes of the meetings of the building committee, newspaper clippings from the *Boston Globe* and letters from President Herbert Hoover and Congresswoman Edith Nourse Rogers.

Among the group of oldest residents was Sarah Pratt, who delivered a history of the old town hall, Atherton W. Rogers, William E. Bills, (the town's lone survivor of the Civil War),

Susan Tourtelett, Elga A. Parmenter, Mrs. Frank Hadley, Caroline B. Way, Samuel Underwood, Sarah A. Hall, Charles Wright, Sylvester D. Perry, Emma A. Ellms, Almira Clark and Ellen Clark.

"The completion of this new hall presents a new problem," said Fairbank in his acceptance speech. "The Selectmen will be called upon to make regulations governing the conduct of affairs which are to be held here. We shall attempt to make these rules stringent enough to preserve the beauty and condition of the hall, yet, at the same time, offer those who use it sufficient freedom and accommodations to carry out their activities successfully."

Fairbank also accepted an American flag from Mrs. Carrie Haynes to fly over the hall. The flag had rested on the casket of her son who died while in the service of his country.

Even as the new hall was nearing completion, Selectmen Fairbank, Howard Goodnow and Borden turned their attention to more serious matters. Noting that there was more truth than poetry in Will Rogers' adage that America was the first nation in the world to go to the poorhouse in an automobile, they challenged town employees to help reduce the escalating tax rate of $29 a thousand by accepting a ten percent pay cut.

Fairbank, a farmer himself, outlined what the depression was doing to the community: "Let us consider what the farmer receives for his goods. From a study of figures recently prepared by the Department of Agriculture we find that today's farmer receives today only 70 percent as much for his products as he did during pre-war time (he was referring to WWI). This comparison of prices applies equally well to most of the basic raw materials sold in the country today."

Fairbank then turned his attention to the public sector: "Another group of workers, and it's a large group too, averaging about one in every eleven, which has been slow to accept an inevitable wage reduction is the army of government and municipal employees. Think of one out of every eleven of us working for the public being supported by taxation at the same rate of wage as in prosperous times, while the people who pay the taxes are receiving wages greatly reduced by the depression.

"Government employees and expenses are increasing every day, and the task of supporting them, which was a serious burden in times of prosperity, has now become intolerable."

The School Committee did not agree, pointing out in its report that "Reckless economy may be more dangerous than reckless spending. The latter may increase taxes and should be avoided if possible, but the former cripples the rising generation and provides a weaker citizenship in the near future." [3]

The Committee grudgingly added that it had dispensed with special instructors in music, art, manual training and sewing in order to live within its greatly reduced appropriation. It also noted that the janitor had taken on the assignment of manual training instructor and that other teachers had increased their workloads.

Principal Alan Flynn pointed out one bright spot: "We have been fortunate in having a small turnover of teachers during the past three years. Our schools may no longer be termed a kindergarten for beginning teachers."

Evidently, the town sided with the Selectmen. The 1932 tax rate dropped $2 to $27 a thousand and remained there for the next four years.

XI
A Skeleton In The Yard

Miss Anne Thorp of Cambridge, granddaughter of Henry Wadsworth Longfellow, and daughter of Annie Allegra Longfellow Thorp--the "Laughing Allegra" of his poem, "The Children's Hour"--came to Sudbury with a dream. She had acquired an old house in Lincoln in 1935 and planned to have it moved and rebuilt on some land she had purchased from the Haynes family on Water Row. When the remodeling was finished, the house, she hoped, would resemble Craigie House, the Cambridge mansion where she grew up.

But first a new cellar hole and foundation had to be dug and laborers were hired. They hadn't been on the job very long when one man was shocked to discover a skull buried barely three feet below the surface of the earth. Chief of Police Seneca W. Hall was summoned along with officers Royal Haynes and Mike Fleming. They carefully exhumed a woman's skeleton, buried face down with no coffin.

The Middlesex County Medical Examiner examined the remains and determined that the woman had died some 60 years previous. No cause of death was determined.

A letter from Clara Ferden, an elderly resident in town, written years later to Becky Fairbank, daughter of long-time Selectman Harvey Fairbank, shed some light on the mystery. Mrs. Ferden stated that the skeleton was probably that of Mary Haynes, daughter of Amos Haynes, janitor and deacon of the Sudbury Methodist Church for many years. She married a man named Turtlott and they had one son. The boy was five years old when Mary "went visiting," and, according to her husband, never returned.

The boy was taken in by Mary's sister, who had married a man named Maynard and resided in the town of the same name. According to Mrs. Ferden, all were still living when the old Haynes place on Water Row was sold to Mrs. Thorp. Turtlott died shortly before the skeleton was discovered.

"Mr. (Elisha) Smith knew Mary and was evidently in love with her when they were both young," wrote Mrs. Ferden. "He would cry when he spoke of her. She married the wrong man and he never married. He died February 26, 1896, and was always a grand old man to us."

Smith left an estate worth $10,995 and two parcels of meadowland on Water Row.

(Material for this chapter came from the 1935 Sudbury Police Log and Clara Ferden's Letter to Becky Fairbank).

XII

Tempest

Wednesday, September 21, 1938, broke still and cloudy. There were signs that the rain of the past three days had finally moved out to sea. At the Wayside Inn, hostesses Priscilla Staples and Muriel DeMille were welcoming back guests who had spent the summer on Cape Cod and the Islands or in New Hampshire, Vermont and Maine. Bob Johnson fired up his touring car for a business trip to Boston. As a breeze picked up in the early afternoon, Barbara Eaton decided to walk up to visit friends near the Wadsworth Cemetery and fly a kite.

There had been warnings on the radio that a tropical storm had hit Miami, Florida, over the weekend, and could possibly be a threat to New England, but nobody paid much attention. The storm had gone out to sea--out of sight, out of mind.

It had been a wet summer in southern New England. By July 25, the total rainfall for Massachusetts was 9.28 inches including a 2.31-inch downpour on the 21st. Rivers and streams were overflowing. The Quabbin and Wachusett reservoirs were full and the earth had absorbed every drop of water that it could handle.

The first kite-flying breezes freshened rapidly and soon leaves and tree branches filled the air. By 4 p.m., it was apparent that the "predicted storm from Miami"--what would come to be called the '38 Hurricane--had arrived.

Guests arriving at the Wayside Inn reported narrowly missing being crushed by falling trees and the roaring of the wind down the ancient fireplaces reminded some of banshee wails. At 5 p.m. the power went out, but the Inn staff was equal to the challenge, breaking out candles and flashlights and making room for transient motorists who sought a place of refuge.

"It was agonizing to watch the trees struggle against the wind," Staples wrote in the Wayside Inn Diary. "The symmetrical maple outside the small dining room fought bravely to survive. The trunk would sway from side to side, then with a swirl of branches and leaves, would right itself again. It seemed like a slender ballet dancer with lacy skirts, swirling, bowing and pirouetting with a final bow from which it did not rise. Its topmost branches brushed the roof of the ball room, but the only damage was a few broken window panes."

The hostesses took turns in the doorway warning visitors coming up the driveway of the danger from fallen trees. A huge Balm of Gilead, after struggling for half an hour, snapped from its base. Mercifully, its towering trunk fell clear of the building, across the driveway onto the lawn toward the East Wing of the Inn. [1]

Leona Johnson recalled cowering with her children in a room called the Den in her old farmhouse on Lancaster Road and watching objects fly past the window. "We saw a man's hat fly by and I said to the kids, 'That looks like Daddy's hat.' That's what it turned out to be. My husband drove all the way from Boston, sometimes cutting across people's lawns to avoid fallen trees." [2]

Mildred Davis Tallant was returning from her daughter's dentist appointment in Hudson when she noticed the wind increase in velocity and broken branches falling on the road. When she returned to her home near Sudbury Center she found a large maple tree that she and her husband had planted in the fall of 1918 fallen across Concord Road. [3]

Phyllis Eaton and Gladys Page were enjoying a well-deserved treat, watching a movie at the Wellesley Theater. When they bought their tickets, the weather was calm and cloudy. When the movie was over, the storm had arrived in full force. [4]

The largest death toll in Sudbury was not human but bovine. The high winds knocked Aubrey Borden's dairy barn off its pinnings. The building collapsed, crushing 50 cows and temporarily trapping three farm hands inside. State police sent ambulances to the scene, but the men were able to escape without serious injury.

The storm departed just as quickly as it had arrived. In the morning the sun shone brightly on a washed-out, cloudless sky. "It was if nothing had happened," wrote Miss Staples, whose cottage was diametrically across Dutton Road from the Redstone school house. "We looked out our window to see if that group of tall, stately pines on the top of the hill (behind the school house where the Martha-Mary chapel now stands) were still standing. No, not one. There was nothing there but a heap of green." [5]

Indeed the huge pines that had covered the knoll were scattered helter-skelter like so many giant jackstraws, some pointing to the east and others to the west. When Henry Ford arrived to survey the damage two weeks later, he decreed that these trees would be used to build a chapel for the Wayside Inn. His instructions were that the building be constructed of material found on the Wayside Inn property by people who lived, worked or went to school there. Aside from the organ, the rugs, the slate roofing, and a crystal chandelier, his wishes were granted.

Ford interrupted his inspection tour to join Wayside Inn Manager Ralph Sennott in a visit to the International Engineering Works in South Framingham, where he purchased a steam boiler to power the Inn's portable sawmill.

"I can't see where the hurricane caused any serious damage in this section," he told the *Sudbury Beacon*. "It just proved the survival of the fittest; took out the weak and left the strong to continue on. We've got hundreds of trees down on these properties, and today, Mr. Sennott and I went to Framingham to buy a boiler for our new sawmill here at Wayside Inn. We're going to put those trees to work.

"New England just needs to wake up to the fact that here is the greatest potential source of living anywhere in the world. These green fields and natural resources make it one of the most desirable places in the world for industry and agriculture."

While the big pines were the first victims because of their short taproots which the winds could pluck out of the ground like so many carrots, other old trees were damaged too. "Everywhere we looked, the lovely old trees were down, their dusty roots exposed to the white, fleecy clouds," Miss Staples remembered. "Everywhere great branches and huge tree trunks were scattered about like fallen nine-pins.

"Here and there were groups of men and boys with axes, but they seemed like midgets trying to cope with what appeared to be a gigantic task. There was a feeling of excitement in the air. Schoolchildren were in the streets shouting and yelling. People were rushing from one spot to another--'See this!! Would you believe that!!' Ohs and Ahs were heard from every direction." [6]

Newspaper reports the morning after revealed the storm's devastation. Six hundred and fifty lives were lost up and down the Eastern Seaboard. Property damage in Sudbury was extensive although the Board of Selectmen reported with pride that all major roads in town were open for traffic the next day.

A survey by Tree Warden Charlie Brackett revealed that 650 trees had been blown down by the storm, 300 more were considered dangerous and 8,000 needed some kind of work. The Boston office of the Works Progress Administration (WPA) immediately assigned all of its workers to hurricane cleanup with no restrictions.

There was good news for many customers of the (Howard) Goodnow and Russell Insurance Agency who had been persuaded to purchase windstorm insurance riders to their fire insurance policies. Two days following the storm, the firm had insurance adjuster Norman R. Crane of Boston in town to settle most claims for hurricane damage on the spot.

It soon became apparent that something had to be done about all the fallen trees. Only so many could be cut up for firewood, a tiresome process that took both labor and time. The federal government assisted by establishing a field sawmill on the farm of Everett Haynes. The mill, owned and operated by the H.K. Operating Company of Sherborn, turned out planks and boards from hurricane timber.

The U.S. Forest Service estimated that enough timber was

knocked down by the storm in New England to build 200,000 five-room houses. Some of the destroyed trees were famous ones, including the Avery Oak in Dedham which was spared in 1796 from being used as timber for the U.S. Frigate Constitution.

Some of the straighter pine logs in South Sudbury were drawn to the vacant lands to the rear of the Goodnow Library where volunteers later constructed a cabin for Sudbury's Boy Scout Troop No. 1 (now Troop 61). Other hurricane timber was milled and used to construct an overnight cabin on Nobscot mountain land donated by Charles O. Parmenter.

Scouting was very much in the news in the fall of 1938 after Loring Smith, son of Mr. and Mrs. Dutee R. Smith of Old Lancaster Road, proved himself a real hero by rescuing fellow scout Charles W. Buzzell Jr. from drowning in Blanford's Pond after their canoe was upset by a gust of wind.

Smith, Buzzell and Roger Thayer of Cambridge had been canoe sailing when the incident occurred. At first they laughed at their predicament and Smith dived to the bottom to free the mast so that the canoe could be righted. Buzzell started to sink in the mud and grabbed Thayer to no avail. By the time Smith resurfaced, Buzzell was stuck in the mud under water.

Smith and Thayer muscled the 160-pound Buzzell to the surface and carried him to the canoe. Sending Thayer for help, Smith commenced the (now outdated) prone method of artificial respiration. By the time the Fire Department arrived with a pulmotor, the rescued boy was breathing faintly. The firemen administered further restoratives and then transported Buzzell, 19, to his home on Framingham Road.

Dr. William Dahill of Wayland was called and, after examination, said that the treatment administered by young Smith had saved his chum's life. Smith, 16, was nominated for and later received the Gold Medal for Saving Life from the National Court of Honor of the Boy Scouts of America.

XIII

Celebration

Charles H. Way of Candy Hill Road was an architect of some renown. A specialist in colonial architecture and design, he had designed and supervised the building of the new Town Hall and many other important structures. But his concern on the morning of Tuesday, July 4, 1939, had nothing to do with architecture.

Way was the chairman of the Tercentenary Committee, charged with the supervision of the celebration of Sudbury's 300th birthday, and the last thing he needed was rain. Down on King Philip Road in South Sudbury, Chief of Police Seneca W. Hall and Chief Marshall Arthur Howe were organizing more than 2,000 marchers, including six drum and bugle corps and more than a dozen floats depicting the history of the town. More than $1,000 of depression-era town money, not to mention hundreds of hours of volunteer work, had been plowed into this birthday party and Way wasn't about to let it be dampened by the weather.

There turned out to be no need for concern. Bright, sunny weather welcomed the celebrants to the culmination of two years of work by Way and his committee, which included Lawrence B. Tighe, John C. Hall, Mary G. Cutler, Jane M. Tufts and Hilda A. Whitney. They had decided upon a three-day celebration spread over the Fourth of July weekend instead of the official anniversary date in September in the hopes that more people would participate.

Way needn't have worried about participation. Just about everyone in town had turned out in home-made grey and white Puritan costumes designed by Mrs. Alan Flynn and Mrs. William Wood for the special church services at the First Parish on Sunday. In keeping with ancient Puritan tradition, a drummer called the faithful--so numerous that an overflow crowd of 500 had to listen to the service from the front lawn of the First Parish Church.

Leading the procession was Selectman Harvey Fairbank, chairman of the newly-formed Board of Appeals, and his wife, followed by a group of direct descendants of original Sudbury settlers including: Ralph Barton, Royal Haynes, Mrs. Carlton Ellms, Robert Hall, William Stone, Caroline Richardson, Miss Josephine Brown, Lucretia Richardson, Mrs. Herbert Newton, Albert Bent, Alvin Noyes, Rev. Channing Brown, Miss Emily Willis, Miss Harriet Goodnow, Miss Emily Thompson, Roland Eaton, Miss Marguerite Fisher, Charles Grout, Ann Bradshaw, Harry Rice, Warren Hunt, Abel Cutting, Chester Perry, Miss Alice Parmenter, Miss Lottie Smith, Everett Bowker, Nancy Fairbank, Roland Cutler Jr. and Marjorie Walker. Chief Eagle Claw and his son Billy, a pair of Sioux Indians, stalked the party of worshipers from a distance.

The old-time, two-part service was capped by a modern sermon preached by the Rev. Frederick Elliot, President of the American Unitarian Association, whose topic was "Faith of Our Fathers." Earlier, Rev. John Madison Foglesong read excerpts from a two-hour diatribe delivered by Puritan minister Jonathan Edwards in 1639.

The men sat on one side of the church and the women across the aisle on the other as in olden times. All were kept in a state of wakefulness by a deacon with a tithing rod, the famed implement with a squirrel tail on one end for the women and a brass knob for wicked boys and sleepy men. Strains of the old colonial hymns such as "Old Hundredth," "The Lord's My Shepherd" and "Rise, God, Judge the Earth in Might," drifted through the open church windows to the crowd outside.

Elliot and Foglesong were assisted by Rev. Leslie Barrett of the Memorial Congregational Church and Methodist minister Elmore Brown as well as Rev. William Channing Browne, a direct descendant of Rev. Edmund Browne who headed the First Parish Church of Sudbury Township from 1640 to 1670. [1]

At the close of the service, families and friends gathered on the church lawn for a picnic just as their ancestors did between sermons at lengthy church services long ago. Many said later that this opportunity to greet old friends from far away was one of the highlights of the weekend.

That afternoon was capped by a visit and short address by Governor Leverett Saltonstall, who called for a revival of the Puritan ideals of good government, before commending the town on its fine community spirit. He said that the Commonwealth was "proud of a town like Sudbury with its background of historic achievements and its present status as a town of homes which are the backbone of the country." [2]

Governor Saltonstall noted that when Sudbury was the center of King Philip's War, his ancestor and namesake, Governor Leverett, was the civil executive of the Colonial Government. His address was followed by the presentation of a stand of silk flags to the Town, a birthday gift from Paul and Clara Ecke, then owners of the Svenks Kaffestuga (now the Lotus Blossom Restaurant) on Route 20.

The revival of 1639 period costumes attracted the attention of three of New York's top fashion designers, who came to Sudbury to observe firsthand the effect of white bonnets and the simple lines of the women's dresses. According to the *Boston Herald* "They made copious notes for which patterns are to be fashioned for use in 1940."

The fact that these 300-year-old styles could be produced so cheaply (one seamstress said that a dress could be made for under $5), and that they were so comfortable in hot weather, roused the interest of the fashion designers. Among the fashion scouts on hand were Miss Hildegard Farrell and Mrs. Gurrell Thomas, both full-time designers for New York fashion houses.

The celebration officially got underway on Saturday when the new Town House was packed to capacity for the performance of two original plays written for the occasion. The Vokes Players of Wayland performed *Thomas Cakebread's Mill* and the Memorial Players of Sudbury followed with *In the Days of 1650* with a cast made up entirely of descendants of original Sudbury settlers.

"Staid Sudbury Flips her Skirts in Lively Tercentenary Dance," announced The *Boston Herald*, reporting on Sudbury's Grand Ball in its July 4th issue. As an incentive to make colonial costumes, the Tercentenary Committee decreed that attendance for the first hour and a half of the Ball would be restricted to those in period costume. More than 300 showed up to dance the old fashioned dances and quadrilles to the call of Albert "Hollywood" Haynes, Henry Ford's dancing master at the Wayside Inn. Haynes was resplendent in purple satin breeches and a pearl-gray coat with 14 purple buttons.

At precisely 11 a.m. on July 4, Chief Hall and his police escort stepped off from the staging area on King Philip Heights (today's Massasoit, Pokonoket and Wilbert Avenues) followed by Chief Marshall Howe and aides Dick Piper and Major Edward Davison, mounted on spirited horses. The colors of Sudbury American Legion Post #191 snapped briskly in the breeze.

Then followed a dozen historic floats chronologically representing important events in the early years of the town. The Sudbury Grange portrayed the first survey of Sudbury meadows in 1633; the Goodman Society presented the purchase of land from Karte, the Indian whom the settlers called "Goodman," with Harry Rice and his money bags stealing the show.

Troop One, Sudbury of the Boy Scouts of America's float depicted the building of the first homes; The Wayside Inn presented the incorporation of the town on September 4, 1639; The Women's Club portrayed the first church in 1642; and the Men's Club recreated the Battle of Green Hill with King Philip's Indians.

Other floats included the first school in 1692, sponsored by the Wayside Inn Boys School; the Sudbury men on the way to Concord on April 19, 1775 by the Kiwanis Club; Peace and Prosperity, sponsored by the Wayland Women's Club and the Wayside Inn stagecoach containing descendants of early settlers Elmer Smith, Frank Goodnow, Harry Cutter, Miss Sarah Pratt, Miss Field and Miss Hiram Haynes.

Following the coach was Dr. George E. Currier in a one-horse chaise and a yoke of oxen with men on foot carrying period farm implements. Also in the line of march were members of the Selectmen, Legion Auxiliary, Red Cross, Public Health Nursing Association, the Sudbury Fire Department with apparatus and fire trucks from the Wayside Inn and the old "Assabet" hand tub.

"There were enough genuine antiques on the float displays to furnish a museum," noted The *Boston Post*. "Then slowly, the history of the progress of the town developed as the floats moved on, like the pages of a book being turned."

A second parade featuring the six drum and bugle corps that would be competing in the afternoon stepped off from South Sudbury at 12:30. Following the competition, the First Corps Cadets Band gave a concert under the leadership of Crawford Anderson. A fireworks display, climaxed by an American Flag set piece, brought the celebration to a close.

Through it all, the town managed to maintain some kind of decorum. Chief Hall and his men had to deal with more than 5,000 automobiles as well as open houses at the Wayside Inn and other old homes in the town, but reported that the celebration was one of the most orderly and law-abiding they had known.

The effects of the Great Depression were still being felt in Sudbury as 1939 came to a close. Henry Ford had renewed his interest in the Parmenter Mill and started work on the Martha-Mary Chapel on the grounds of the Wayside Inn, but the mill deal, known by Ford interests as the Wash Brook Project, never materialized and the chapel construction was limited to Ford's employees and the students at the Wayside Inn Boys School.

But the end to the hard times was in sight, although the price would be high. On September 3, 1939, Great Britain declared war on Nazi Germany. Sudbury men would soon be fighting for their country once more, but this time, the battlefields would be halfway round the world.

The Barton Place

Some folks in town remember Ralph Barton and call his farm on Old Marlborough Road "Ralph Barton's place," but the old timers know better. To them it's "the Barton Place." Ralph was just the last care-taker of a family that goes back for more than a century.

The old white farmhouse goes back further than that. It was built in 1817 by Israel Hunt and generations of Bartons have lived there since. They ran a little up-and-down sawmill by the brook beyond the house and held patriotic celebrations on Liberty Ledge nearby, but mostly they farmed, and the green fields, high stone walls and neat buildings bear witness to their skill.

The old barns were rebuilt by neighbors in 1847 after a tramp had started a fire in one of them while trying to keep warm on a cold winter's night. Three barns and 17 head of cattle were destroyed. The ashes had hardly stopped smoking when fellow townsfolk started coming by with boards, nails and offers of assistance. Inside the barns today you will find boards with the names of their donors still clearly visible.

As former town historian John Powers once observed, the Barton Place is a symbol of all the values of serenity. It is an old place and a peaceful place, a place not suited for tract houses or high-speed traffic. It is a place worth keeping as it always was which the Town, in its wisdom, has done. It is the Town's "Home Place" and hopefully it always will be.

The '40s

Controversy, Gold Stars, The U.N. and a School

The decade of the 1940s began and ended in controversy. The question of whether or not town employee Ellsworth Tebo was at fault in the accidental death of Alfred John Kalilianen on Haynes Road cost veteran Chief of Police Seneca W. Hall his job and pitted much of the town against the Selectmen. Following World War II and a spurned bid by the United Nations to locate its world headquarters in town, Sudbury began to feel the first effects of the baby boom and agonized over the construction of a modern school facility.

Along the way veteran Superintendent of Schools Frank Benedict retired after 30 years of service to the town and was replaced by Alfred R. Kenyon and later, in 1944, by Owen B. Kiernan who went on to distinguish himself as one of the state's top educators.

The Pequod District of the Boy Scouts of America dedicated their new log cabin, built of hurricane lumber, behind the Goodnow Library and the federal government took several homes in West Sudbury by eminent domain for an ammunition dump.

In 1942, Alfred Meissner of Athol became the town's first full-time chief of police at a salary of $2,050; Leavitt Road was renamed Maple Avenue; the town rented the Hosmer House for $750 to be used as a teacher's lodge for single women; L. Roy Hawes's heifer "Libby" returned home three days after being sold to a farmer in an adjoining town; the Board of Appeals granted permission for "Squire" Wilfred Allen, a graduate of Henry Ford's Wayside Inn Boys School, to open a country store in the old Sudbury Pines Dance Hall building (now the site of the Sudbury Pines Rehab facility) and the Bell Telephone Company took over operation of the telephone system from Mr. and Mrs. Lawrence Tighe, necessitating a change in the fire alarm system.

Alton Clark lost to Aubrey Borden in the 1946 Selectmen's race by six votes; Clyde Barber was appointed Special Police Officer for Duty at Town Dump and the selectmen warned of the danger that increasing tax rates would drive residents out of town. In the 1948 Town Report, Forrest Bradshaw noted that the clock in the steeple of the First Parish Church is the property of the Town.

According to Bradshaw, 110 subscribers put up money or materials to buy and install the clock on November 8, 1871. Isaac Clark donated $40 worth of lumber (a considerable sum in the nineteenth century) and Dalphon Osborn turned out the dials in his shop. The Town is on record as paying for repairs and upkeep as early as 1872 and '73.

Boston Edison's announcement of a 110,000-volt overhead power line through East Sudbury sent Sudbury, Wayland and Lincoln scurrying to hire counsel. It would be more than two decades before the issue was finally settled. International politics found its way into town as High School Principal Alan F. Flynn ended his annual report with a strong anti-Communist message.

And, in a preface to the 1949 Town Report, Harvey Fairbank, writing for the Board of Selectmen, summed up the last 50 years and took a glimpse at the future:

> The year 1949 marks the end of another half century in the life of the citizens of Sudbury and perhaps a few reflections and observations may be appropriate in this report," he wrote.
>
> At the turn of the century, the population was between 1,100 and 1,200 with a large proportion of the land owned by farmers with large holdings of personal property in the form of livestock. This class of people carried most of the tax burden.
>
> True, the tax levy was nothing compared to what it is today, yet it was a hardship for many to meet their taxes then. It is today. Some of us can remember that taxes were abated, donations from the charity funds given, and other relief was used to keep citizens from 'going to the poor house.'

It was the 'horse and buggy' era with the citizens reasonably content with their country life and limited services which the voters felt they could afford. They received no doles from the state or the federal government with their directives and formulas. They were masters of their own destinies, for all practical purposes, unhampered and largely uncontrolled by state and federal laws.

We have come a long way during those 50 years. We are no longer the suburban village far removed from the city. We are a part of the metropolitan area. Our population has doubled, it is true, yet the cost of government has increased several times. The population is now made up principally of people of moderate means with businesses or occupations elsewhere.

In these 50 years, we have experienced periods of inflation and periods of depression, and will continue to do so in the future. During all these periods there has been an ever-increasing centralization of government control and power with ever-increasing government agencies and services...The effect and cost of this centralization has terrifically accelerated in the last two decades...It is like a high powered automobile with no brakes...It might be wise for us to 'consider well our situation,' before we forget how to use the brakes.

XIV

Controversy

The Friday, February 23, 1940, edition of the *Sudbury Beacon* gave a detailed account on Page One, being very careful not to place blame:

Alfred John Kalilianen of Mossman Road, N. Sudbury was killed early Sunday [February 18] morning in an accident involving a town truck near the junction of Haynes and Old Marlborough Roads. The truck was the big International with V-shaped snowplow attached and driven by Ellsworth Tebo of Boston Post Road. With him were Ray Hartwell and Horatio Whitney.

The crew had completed the snow removal on Haynes Road and was headed for Sudbury when hailed by a car which had brought Kalilianen from Maynard. The truck stopped until Kalilianen had crossed the road in front. It had gone only a few yards when the accident happened.

While Inspector Robert Huddy of the Registry and Chief [Seneca W.] Hall have not completed their investigation, it is believed the deceased may have attempted to jump on the truck and either slipped, striking his head against the body of the vehicle or was caught by the chains on the rear wheel so as to be flung against the truck. His skull was fractured and his neck broken..." [1]

"Johnny" Kalilianen was a popular figure in North Sudbury with the reputation of a strong and tireless worker who enjoyed a drink or two on Saturday nights. Besides helping out his parents and brothers on the home farm off Route 117, he had worked part-time for the highway department and knew most of the employees there.

Chief Hall knew that he was dealing with a hot potato as soon as he got the call at his home in South Sudbury. A town vehicle and town employees were involved and the town had not yet had the forethought to take out liability insurance. He decided to ask Huddy, an old colleague and one of the Registry's top photographers, to join the investigation. By the time they had arrived at the scene near the junction of Haynes and Old Marlborough Roads, Dr. George E. Currier had pronounced Kalilianen dead of a broken neck.

Currier, Huddy and Hall examined and photographed the footprints and tire tracks and took statements from all but one of the witnesses. All agreed that Tebo, driving the town truck with Whitney sitting in the passenger seat operating the snowplow and Hartwell standing in the body spreading sand, had been flagged down by Garnet Bennett of Weston, the driver of a Chevrolet motor coach, near the intersection of Haynes and Old Marlborough Roads.

Besides Bennett and Kalilianen, the car contained Margaret and Georgani Guilme of Waltham and an undertaker named Walsh. The Guilmes stated that Kalilianen alighted from the back seat, crossed the road, and asked Tebo for a lift. When Tebo declined, Kalilianen crossed in front of the plow and disappeared. The truck moved forward a few feet and Kalilianen's dead body was discovered in back of the rear wheels.

Tebo claimed he had no conversation with Kalilianen who allegedly crossed in front of the plow before Tebo put the truck in second gear and started ahead. A records check disclosed that Tebo's driver's license had been suspended for five days before being reinstated on January 9, 1940. [2]

In his more than 45 years as a police officer, Chief Hall had dealt with many fatal automobile accidents, but this one would come back to haunt him. In the ensuing months, the Kalilianen family brought suit against the town, and when Hall and Huddy were deposed, their account of the evidence as they saw it indicated that Tebo was at fault. This testimony enraged Selectmen John C. Hall, Lawrence Tighe and Everett D. Haynes, who were struggling with a rapidly rising tax rate. The duty of the police department was to support the Town, not cost it money.

Matters came to a head on December 5, 1941 when Chief Hall

was summoned to a Selectmen's meeting and asked to resign "for the good of the town." He refused and immediately retained John P. Driscoll of Framingham as his attorney. In the closed-door meeting, Hall was told that he didn't cooperate with the heads of the Fire and Highway departments, didn't enforce traffic laws, would not direct traffic at official town functions unless invited and, according to Board Secretary John C. Hall, "his conduct of matters involving possible liability to the town was not in the town's best interests."

On December 11, 1941, the Selectmen made it official. Hall was fired and replaced by Tighe amidst the protests of 280 citizens who signed a petition demanding a public hearing on the matter, which was slated for December 29. [3]

Charlie Way asked Hall to call off the hearing "for the best interests of the town" and sign a paper to that affect, but Hall didn't like the wording of the document and refused. The following evening at the Town Hall, J.C. Hall and Tighe found themselves facing an angry crowd of more than 300 which got even angrier when J.C. Hall wasted the first hour of the meeting reading the names of all the petitioners and then tried to deny Chief Hall his right to counsel.

Tighe added other charges to those made during the December 5 Selectmen's meeting. He alleged that Chief Hall stopped a fire engine on the way to a fire to check William Davison's driver's license. Hall countered that the check was made back at the firehouse after the fire was extinguished.

Tighe also charged that the Chief didn't prevent the State Police from questioning Fire Chief Ethan Davison regarding a break-in at the Water District Pumping Station. Driscoll scornfully asked the Selectmen if they expected Chief Hall to prevent a witness from giving information to law enforcement officers. [4]

"I've known that the Selectmen were gunning for me for some time," Chief Hall told The *Sudbury Beacon* on January 9, 1942. "But regardless of what they claim, I have served the best interests of the town for the past 45 years. During that time,

Sudbury has been quiet, a respectable, law-abiding town with relatively few breaks or disorders of any kind.

"I know the Selectmen have no basis for their charges. Why they went back to the early nineteen-twenties to trump up charges against me--charges which have no foundation whatsoever--is beyond me."

Whether the charges were just or not didn't matter. The selectmen pointed out that Chief Hall was an appointed official who could be removed by them at will. At the March 1942 Town Meeting the selectmen threw him a bone, sponsoring a warrant article to: "Retire and put on the pension rolls under provision of the General Laws, Chapter 321, Section 85, Seneca W. Hall, including the appropriation of $500 for such pension for the coming year." Later the town voted to make the pension retroactive to January 1, 1942.

In the end it was Chief Hall who had the last laugh. On December 7, 1945, the heirs of Alfred John Kalilianen were awarded $5,624.40 in damages from the town. Hall testified for the plaintiffs.

XV

Eight Gold Stars

In Memoria
They are not dead, our sons who fell in glory
Who gave their lives for freedom and for truth
We shall grow old, but never their great story
Never their gallant youth

In a perpetual springtime set apart
Their memory forever green shall grow
In some bright secret meadow of the heart
Where never falls the snow.

--Joseph Auslander

The Honor Roll stood clear and white against the Mount Pleasant hillside, halfway between the First Parish and Methodist (now Presbyterian) churches. From across the street in the Town Hall the sound of singing floated across the Common. After a brief silence a solemn group of Sudbury residents, led by the American Legion color guard, filed to the Honor Roll and formed a semicircle in front of it.

Dorothy and Madeline Quinn stepped to the Roll and drew back the curtains that draped it, revealing the list of 171 Sudbury soldiers, sailors and Marines who were serving in World War II. Five of those names, including that of their brother, Leo Quinn, had gold stars next to them. Before the Japanese finally surrendered on August 14, 1945, there would be three more. Ironically, the family of Albert Spiller, the last to die, would be notified on V-E Day, May 7, 1945.

The War came to Sudbury quietly. Most people heard of the bombing of Pearl Harbor over the radio. At the Wayside Inn, hostess Priscilla Staples brought the radio into the Old Bar Room so that guests and staff could hear President Franklin Delano Roosevelt's "Day of Infamy" speech to a joint session of Congress. The playing of The Star Spangled Banner followed and all in the room rose to their feet. Little did they know then that Wayside Inn Boys School graduate Ernest Flynn would give his life in the jungles of Saipan and that five other graduates would also make the supreme sacrifice.

Civil Defense preparation began immediately. Director Charlie Way implemented air raid contingency plans already in place in conjunction with Red Cross disaster units and submitted a detailed, three-page summary in the 1941 Town Report.

Way established a Report Center in a large office in the Town Hall which would be staffed by the chairman, a secretary, a telephone operator, the principal division directors and the chief air raid wardens. The center was to receive all warnings from the Framingham Control Center and local wardens, and issue instructions to various defense sectors. During an air raid alert, it would have supreme command of all activities. Police, firemen, road repair crews and Civil Defense building rescue crews were based near the center in order to respond quickly to any emergency.

The Protection Division, commanded by Clifton Giles, appointed male and female air raid wardens for all sectors of the town. Each sector was divided into patrol areas and patrol wardens were empowered to check completeness of blackout as well as citizen observation of air raid regulations, and observe any damage done in their areas by enemy action.

Elsewhere, Gertrude M. Halleron, Director of the Blackout Committee, distributed pamphlets to every family in town, giving instructions for blacking out of all buildings, while Evacuation Director Albert E. Haynes laid plans for the housing of evacuees from Boston or other coastal communities in the event of a German air attack.

Dr. George E. Currier of North Sudbury directed the Medical Division, which maintained two first aid stations in the lower Town Hall and at the Nursing Association rooms along with a mobile first aid station and two ambulances. His staff included two doctors, six registered nurses and numerous qualified first aid workers.

The possibility of a German air attack was taken quite seriously throughout the region. Alerts were to be broadcast from the Framingham Control Center to local officials, but the general public would be warned only if the threat of a raid in the local area became imminent. Continuous sounding of the fire siren at Sudbury Center, fire and police car sirens and church bells would be used to spread the alarm.

Meanwhile, Sudbury men and women were signing up for the service. One of the first to go was Frank Bastinelli of North Sudbury, who would also become the town's first casualty. He was killed in action at Guadacanal on November 22, 1942.

"He was a town boy who grew up, went to school and worked here. He gave his all that we might go on living in peace and freedom in the home he loved so well," eulogized *Sudbury In World War II*, a publication of the Sudbury Red Cross sent to local servicemen all over the world.

Bastinelli was born in Maynard in 1916 and was brought to Sudbury by his father and mother, Victor and Margerita Bastinelli, in 1917. Frank attended the Sudbury public schools and later worked for Gordan Hunter, Commissioner of Roads, who spent the war building airfields in China. One of Bastinelli's buddies sent a picture of his grave and its marker to his family.

By 1943, nearly 200 Sudbury men and women were in uniform all over the world and the American Legion and Red Cross combined forces to publish a monthly newsletter filled with the news of home and of friends in the service. The town voted $750 to rent the Hosmer House for a year and turn it into a lodge for single female teachers.

"We could not have kept some of our good teachers without providing a homelike place near the school where they can live," the School Committee explained in the *1944 Sudbury Town Report*. "We are depending on the lodge to help fill present vacancies and to keep the staff at full strength next year."

In January of 1944, the War Department brought more bad news. On January 3, Seaman Second Class Milton Truman

Williams was killed in an explosion at sea. His work aboard ship was with the radar equipment which he had previously helped to make at the Raytheon Plant in Waltham. His remains were not recovered.

Williams' wife remembered his humor. "He wrote home of picking up a pip (target) while on radar watch--something ominous floating in the sea. The ship was brought to general quarters and all guns were trained. The searchlight was finally turned on to reveal a seagull perched on a floating orange crate and blinking at the light."

"That he could laugh and still get on with the job marked him as a real American fighting man," wrote Mrs. Vivian "Sue" Fletcher, editor of the *American Legion Newsletter*. "It is what the Germans cannot seem to understand, but what they are finding out to their sorrow...that because a man can joke and make light of danger doesn't mean he's not a real he-man. Milton gave the Germans plenty to think about and Sudbury will always remember him with gratitude."

Disillusionment with military life came quickly to Algy Alexander when he arrived at Sampson Naval Training station for his boot training. Algy chose the Navy "because sailors don't have to march." But they do, Algy quickly discovered, and how. What did you expect boots were for?" somebody wanted to know.

At least one Sudbury business was directly involved in the war effort. Lefty Mullins wrote from Africa that "Skeeter Skats," made by Herb Atkinson's Sudbury Laboratory, worked well on local mosquitoes that he described as small but tough.

Sudbury bought a whopping 205.7 percent of its war bond quota and disbanded the State guard company because of insufficient enrollment to meet state requirements. Seventeen members joined the armed forces, three more transferred into other government services and six went to work for war plants.

Sudbury also went to town in the salvage campaigns. Over 80 tons of scrap metal, 6,500 pounds of tin cans, seven tons of old tires, 50,000 pounds of fats and 14 tons of waste paper were collected for war industry. In the fall of the year, children were asked to collect and dry milkweed pods. The floss within the pods was needed to provide the flotation fiber in badly-needed life preservers.

Every effort was made to encourage townspeople to avoid telling their troubles to the troops overseas and, instead, send news of the family and the town. Mrs. Fletcher set the tone in the May 1944 *American Legion Newsletter* with a description of spring in Sudbury:

"The grass is growing green in front of the white Town Hall. Daffodils blow bravely by the low, gray stone walls on Maynard Road. Frogs peep in the April dusk in the ponds on Old Town (Sudbury) Road. Fifteen thousand cabbages were set out yesterday at the Hazen Davis Farm and, for the last two nights, our pup has gone AWOL. It's still cold enough to wear a sweater at sunny noon...but spring has come."

Ramona Davis of North Sudbury was named Emergency Farm Labor Assistant for the Middlesex County Extension Service. Her gang of 37 high school and college girls was responsible for the 15,000 cabbages and sent 250 bushels of produce a day to market during the growing season. [1]

Throughout 1944, a controversy raged in town over whether or not to consolidate the Wayland and Sudbury high schools for the duration of the war. The School Committee, composed of Maxwell Eaton, Dorothy Piper and Al Gardner, approved the concept, noting that more and better teachers would be available; a modern building with gymnasium and athletic fields was available at Wayland; a greater variety of subjects would be included in the curriculum; larger classes would provide more competition and better opportunity for the average student, and a consolidated school would be more economical.

Opposing factions countered that the Wayland school building was inadequate and that Sudbury might lose jurisdiction over the educational program. Besides, they said, the majority of Wayland students and parents are opposed to the idea anyway.

The uproar filled the Town Hall at the 1944 Annual Town

Meeting and it was finally decided to select a committee of seven citizens of Sudbury to investigate and settle the matter. Forrest Bradshaw, L. Roy Hawes, Mrs. James Bartlett, Harvey Fairbank, Francis McGettigan, Arthur Howe and Mrs. Richard Burkes were chosen. At a special Town Meeting in early April the Committee of Seven recommended against the consolidation by a 6-1 margin, with only Mr. Howe dissenting. It took another Town Meeting, but the concept was finally voted down.

"Even though the proposed merger fell through, it has brought about one positive result," noted *The American Legion Newsletter*, "There has not been, for a long time, as much interest in and discussion of our school situation as these past few weeks. Let us hope the active interest will continue and bear good fruit." [2]

Word came in May that First Sergeant Hale Very, who enlisted from Sudbury in 1942, had been confirmed killed in action November 27, 1943. Very, a music instructor at St. Mark's School in Southborough, had been reported missing in action.

Word of the Normandy invasion reached Sudbury over the radio in the early morning of June 6, 1944, bringing the Town its fourth and fifth casualties. Roger Thayer, brought up and educated in Sudbury before moving to Somerville, was killed during the invasion as was Leo Quinn.

Quinn's loss hit the town hard. His father Leo Quinn Sr. was a firefighter and town official and everybody knew him. He played high school sports and was a popular member of the Class of 1942. His pro burial mass at St. Bridget's Church in Maynard was packed and, at the Halleron home in Sudbury, the American flag that had been brought back from World War I was flown at half mast.

"He died that we might live," wrote Mrs. Fletcher. "But in a larger sense, he will never cease to walk our roads and lanes. He and the other Sudbury boys who have gone from here, not to return with their packs and guns, have joined that larger group, beginning with the brave men of the Revolution and coming down through the years, who have fought to make Sudbury and our nation what they are."

There was a subtle feeling in town on D-Day that perhaps this was the beginning of the end. The doors of the First Parish Church were thrown open for any who cared to come and citizens from all creeds dropped in to pray and take a turn at ringing the ancient bell which had been installed two centuries before when George Washington was president.

"I've wanted for years to ring that bell and now I have," Bea Cutting remarked. "Somehow it was fitting that on that day when all our thoughts and prayers were overseas with our men that the bell which has called our people to prayer for more than 200 years, should peal again."

In the evening, Mrs. Charles Capon added to the solemnity to the scene by playing old hymns on the organ. Many church members acted as custodians including, among others, Mrs. Stuart Edgerly, Miss Harriet Goodnow and Mrs. Cutting.

Two more casualties followed that summer. On July 4, Wayside Inn Boys School graduate PFC Ernest Flynn of the U.S. Marine Corps Reserve was killed in action at Saipan. [3]

A month later on August 3, Cpl. Edmund Barrett of Concord Road in North Sudbury, was reported missing in action. Barrett was listed as lost in the sinking of a transport in the Mediterranean. [4]

Not all the reports from the war zone were sad. Harrison Bennett reported from his post on a PT Boat somewhere near New Guinea that, laundry facilities being few, he put his clothes on the end of a line and dragged them behind the boat to wash them. Imagine his horror when he discovered that the line had broken and his clothes were gone. "And now," Bennett wrote home plaintively, "I haven't any pants."

The Fletchers, Pete Eaton and Forrest Bradshaw saw to it that the happenings in Sudbury were quickly spread around the world by the *Legion Newsletter*. The January 1945 issue carried this account:

The tree in front of Town Hall was lighted again in honor of all the veterans home on leave. Nobody went hungry on Christmas day although some who went optimistically to the butcher's for a turkey or goose generally came home with a roasting chicken.

Cranberry sauce soared into astronomical blue (ration) points and butter and bacon just weren't. So we brought out the cans from our last summer's victory gardens and beamed when the guests insisted they'd never tasted such tomato juice! Neither had we. The sweat of our brows tasted sweet. Every veteran able to leave Cushing [Veterans] Hospital had an invitation for Christmas.

We missed the Santa Claus on the roof of the Wayside Inn and the usual pageant there, but they were discontinued for the duration because of lack of gas for the audience to get there. But the school children sang carols lustily. The Congregational Church gave a pageant on Christmas Eve as many were able to walk there and many homes were open for neighborhood sings and greetings.

It was a white Christmas with snow crunching underfoot and, on the roads, icy driving. In spite of the weather, many attended Midnight Mass on Christmas Eve and communion on Christmas morning. One British sailor guest explained: "I promised my wife that I'd go to Christmas morning early service and she promised that she'd be there too and so, though she's in England and I'm here, we'll be together.

And so were you and we together as we prayed that these wartime Christmases would soon be over and that all of you would soon be home again for the birthday of the Prince of Peace in 1945. [5]

The Town's eighth and final casualty was perhaps the saddest of all. On April 11, 1945, one day before President Roosevelt died at Warm Springs, Georgia, Albert Spiller was killed in action while serving with General George Patton's Third Army. A letter from his chaplain related that Albert was killed while carrying ammunition for the heavy machine gun which was covering a withdrawal from Haagen, Germany. He is buried in an American cemetery in Germany. His parents were notified on V-E Day, May 7, 1945.

"That word of Albert's death came on V-E day was both sober-ing and saddening because it reminded us of the cost of that day...that it has been bought with blood and tears," Mrs. Fletcher wrote in the *Legion Newsletter*. "This is America at its best. Its sacrifices make it more imperative that we insist that the peace to come must be worthy of the price that Albert and other Sudburyites have paid."

Sudbury mourned FDR's death with the rest of the world. The First Parish church bell was tolled 63 times. Formal memorial services followed in the Congregational Church. [6]

The formal end to the war in Europe was a bittersweet day for Sudbury. The sobering news of Spiller's death was somewhat tempered by a telegram from "Red" Kendall who was released from a POW camp in Germany and was on his way home. Aside from a thanksgiving service at the First Parish, there was lit-tle celebration. The war in the Pacific and the lives of Sudbury soldiers, sailors and Marines fighting there were on everyone's minds.

There were no fireworks on the Fourth of July, 1945. Those were reserved for the time when the boys would come march-ing home again, but there was a parade and the July issue of the *Legion Newsletter* carried a blow-by-blow description. [7]

Deep thankfulness and then a spontaneous burst of celebration marked V-J Day, August 14, 1945. All the organizations in town, headed by the town fathers, joined the rejoicing. The young people hosted the town at a dance at the Town Hall and Len Stiles drove his coal truck all over town carrying an impromptu orchestra containing just about every musical instrument known to man. The sound they made was more enthusiastic than musical, but at that point nobody really cared.

The real celebration took place two days later. A thanksgiving service at the First Parish Church was followed by a mile-long parade marshalled by George Mailley and headed by veterans home on leave and the American Legion. Behind them, a motorcade of some 60 vehicles representing every organization in town celebrated the fact that, not only was the war over, but rationing was off!

As the parade wound its way past the Town Hall and gathered around the Honor Roll at the top of the Common, the mood turned somber. Rev. Dr. J. Carroll Morris, Minister of the Congregational Church offered a prayer and Coast Guard Lt. Commander William C. Mahoney delivered a short, but inspiring talk.

Then the crowd broke up, some to watch the ball games at the high school field or listen to a band concert, and others to dance on the green or sit on the Town Hall steps and take in the scene. Sue Fletcher heard one of the town's oldest residents remark: "I've never seen so many people completely happy."

XVI

The World At Our Back Door

Dr. Stoyal Gavrilovic of Yugoslavia alighted from a State Police cruiser, climbed to the top of the fire tower on Nobscot Mountain and uttered the words that would send chills up the back of many Sudbury landowners:

"We may be looking at the spot where man finally will achieve enduring peace and where all injustices to men will be corrected without conflict," he said.

Gavrolic and the six men with him were members of the United Nations Organization's (UNO) Site Selection Committee. Their whirlwind visit by blimp and motor car to Sudbury and the South Middlesex region on January 19 and 20, 1946, was meant to explore the possibility of locating the UN's permanent headquarters here.

Sudbury seemed to have everything the UNO wanted. It was close to the academic and medical centers of Boston, yet not too close. A world-class airport, already being used by international transport planes, was available at nearby Bedford, and the rural nature of the area lent itself to the atmosphere of tranquility that the organization sought for its deliberations.

And there was another criterion that Gavrilovic and his committee felt was of the utmost importance. The Sudbury-Concord-Marlborough-Lincoln area was rural enough so that the UNO's 40 to 50 square mile facility would displace "only 2,100" persons. Other sites under consideration by the committee would require the displacement of many more.

Following the Nobscot trip, Gavrilovic told reporters at a Wayside Inn luncheon of old-fashioned chicken pie that two separate sites were under consideration, one in Lincoln and another in Marlborough. Because these overlapped and covered an area of 70 square miles, Gavrilovic intimated that the

UNO would settle for a 40- to 50-square mile area in between the two, placing the proposed headquarters buildings somewhere near the Wayside Inn. "The ground is excellent for construction and there are many other desirable features," he said. [1]

While columnists in the Boston newspapers trumpeted the region's virtues, some citizens of Sudbury took an entirely different tack. Even as the Committee, shepherded by Governor Maurice Tobin, climbed aboard a Navy blimp at the South Weymouth Naval Air Station for an aerial tour of the site on January 20, 200 townspeople, a quarter of them returned servicemen, signed a petition directing the Selectmen to voice the town's opposition to the UNO complex to Governor Tobin as soon as possible.

Selectmen Francis McGettigan, Lawrence Tighe and Aubrey Borden denied having any contact at all with the United Nations, but did arrange a question-and-answer session with the Massachusetts UNO Committee.

At the same time, a citizens group was attacking from another direction, composing a strong letter telling the UNO Sight Selection Committee in words of one syllable that the organization was not welcome in Sudbury. A few days later, groups from other neighboring towns followed suit.

Sudburyites had every reason to be concerned about displacement. Early in WWII the government took over 3,000 acres of land in the town's northwest corner (the Fort Devens Annex which is now part of the Great Meadows National Wildlife Refuge), evicting residents and paying them an arbitrary price for their land. Mr. and Mrs. Richard C. Hill of Candy Hill Road had been among the few Sudbury residents to have their house and land taken and were afraid that the advent of a UNO headquarters here would trigger a similar exodus on a larger scale.

"We got all excited," Hill told *The Middlesex Daily News* in 1985. "It looked as if they were going to take over the whole town and everyone was going to be evicted." The signers of the petition were conspicuous by their absence from the meeting with Massachusetts UNO Committee members Orson Adams Jr.,

Professor G. Holmes Perkins and Christian Science Monitor Managing Editor Erin D. Canham on January 30. Those that did attend, expressed their concern in two words: "How much?"

Professor Perkins pointed out that Sudbury had a relatively low assessment valuation--$3,680,000--and a tax rate of $31 which meant that a parcel worth $1,000 here might be worth twice as much in neighboring Wayland. All transactions would be between willing buyers and willing sellers, he added. Any disputes over land values would be settled by the courts to everyone's satisfaction.

The Committee revealed that construction of the permanent headquarters would require at least three years with 1,300 persons on hand the first year, 2,000 the second and up to 3,000 when the project was completed. While construction was taking place, the UNO would operate from a 200-acre temporary site near Boston.

"The UNO Project is one of the most magnificent and challenging opportunities that has ever come to the United States," added Canham. "It would mean that two to three thousand of the world's greatest experts in the field of diplomacy would come here. A meeting of the General Assembly once a year would bring the cream of the world."

Meanwhile, the protestors themselves were coming under fire from another front. A letter to the editor of *The Boston Globe*[2] laced them for their bad manners:

> To the Editor--The vast majority of the citizens of Sudbury, both the descendants of the original settlers and those who have settled in this community during the more recent past since the Civil War, protest emphatically against the display of bad manners given by certain local citizens in affronting the state UNO Committee, the government of the Commonwealth and the distinguished guests of our nation, the UNO Committee on Sites itself.
>
> We hope that the 50 nations associated with our beloved country in this enterprise of peace will not judge our historic community by this action or assume that it represents the old New

England courtesy of our people.

This whole agitation is the work of local land barons who do not seem to care about the future prosperity of our town any more than they care about its repute for generosity or good neighborliness toward visitors. What an example to give to our youth!!

What an insult to the sons of Sudbury who served in the war for human freedom and now return to find a group of stuffy, middle-aged standpatters who didn't fight the war trying to destroy what the dead died for!--A Group of Sudbury Citizens

In the end it was not Sudbury, but the National Knights of Columbus meeting in Boston that nixed the UNO headquarters project once and for all. The K of C denounced "Godless Russia" and its part in the United Nations Experiment. Soviet Union delegate Gorgi Saksin was so incensed that he refused to consider any site in Massachusetts. When the matter finally came up for a vote, the Russians and Scandinavians supported New York while Great Britain held firm for Massachusetts.

What finally turned the tide for New York and the site that the U.N. currently occupies was an $8.5 million grant from John D. Rockefeller Jr. to purchase an 18-acre site on the East River, leaving Sudbury wondering just what might have been.

XVII

$550,000 For A School??

Superintendent of Schools Owen B. Kiernan laid it on the line in words of one syllable in the *1947 Town Report*. If Town Meeting refused to come up with money for a new school building by 1948, he would double up on classes or go for a two-session day.

The unthinkable was happening in Sudbury. With the war over, young couples with kids were moving into town and building new houses at an unprecedented rate. King Philip Heights in South Sudbury became the town's first housing development and, if the projections were right, by 1948, there wouldn't be room enough in the Center School building for everyone.

The Sudbury Parent-Teachers Association (PTA) was also making loud noises, pointing out that the schools were facing a critical post-war period due to "lapsed public interest and support" as well as increasing costs and a shortage of teachers. Buildings and programs, they said, were unchanged and out of date.

"Just as townspeople organized for civil defense in wartime emergency," the PTA suggested, "they could also organize in peace in defense of our way of life. To pass on the best we can find through the education of our children."

Noting that the pay scale for teachers in Sudbury was average for Massachusetts, the Association proposed raising salaries-- already 61 percent of the school budget--in order to attract and keep better teachers.

Things were already crowded in 1946. The ground floor of the White Building housed grades one through six while the upstairs handled Junior High and High School classes. There were no gymnasium facilities. Two classrooms at the South School on Massasoit Avenue took some pressure off the lower grades and sixteen more youngsters attended the Redstone School at the Wayside Inn, where Henry Ford picked up the tab and threw lunch and dancing lessons into the bargain.

It wasn't until the March 1948 Town Meeting that the matter came to a head. The School Committee submitted an article proposing an elementary school with gymnasium and auditorium which would cost the town $550,000. Faced with a $47 per thousand tax rate already, residents immediately voted the proposal down, opting instead for a $15,000 appropriation for a complete set of plans and the appointment of a special building committee to oversee the process. Dr. Howard Emmons, a professor at Harvard University who had recently acquired the old Hurlbut Parsonage on Concord Road, was named chairman.

Emmons delivered his committee's report at a Special Town Meeting on June 7, 1948, and offered the town four options, ranging from a bare-bones, six-room, one-story building with no gymnasium, to a 12-room, two story edifice with a gym-auditorium. The town voted 194-6 to raise $285,000 for a 12-room, one-story building with gym-auditorium to be built on town land to the rear of the Center School.

Town Meeting then voted to continue the work of the committee until firm bids were obtained and reported to the town. It was nearly a year before the Permanent Building Committee, as it was now called, requested an additional $180,000 in addition to the $300,000 already appropriated so that construction could begin.

The Committee got the money, but not before a floor fight at a special town meeting on February 16, 1949. After a request for a secret ballot was voted down, the Town voted 310-95 to appropriate the funds and let the committee get on with its work. In a related article, the Meeting instructed the committee to use red brick in the building's construction.

By now the tax rate had ballooned to $50 per thousand and Superintendent Kiernan was predicting that the school population would peak in 1956. He was wrong.

Fourteen bids were ultimately received, with S. Volpe and Co. Inc. the lowest at $395,989 for the entire project or 68.5 cents a cubic foot. Emmons noted that when state aid was factored in, the school would raise the tax rate by 9 percent to $54 per thousand.

The Committee concluded its work on October 30, 1950. when it accepted the building from contractor S. Volpe and Co. for $480,600.30, just $600.33 over budget. Emmons proudly pointed out that the town would be reimbursed $144,720 by the State in payments of $7,236 annually over the next 20 years.

As Emmons and his committee did its work, the town was moving on other fronts to keep the housing developments from getting out of hand. The Planning Board considered the first subdivision plan in 1946 and turned down a proposal for a business district. The 1949 Town Meeting established several new business zones and approved a by-law change that would limit building permits to two years.

Other zoning by-laws had been in place since 1939, but Sudbury would soon discover that they were hopelessly out of date.

Martha-Mary Chapel

The sixth and last chapel built by Henry Ford and named in honor of his and his wife's mothers, Martha Ford and Mary Bryant, the Martha-Mary Chapel was constructed from timber knocked down by the 1938 Hurricane. Ford decreed that the chapel be built from materials available on the Wayside Inn estate by people who lived, worked or went to school there. Much of the labor was provided by students of the Wayside Inn Boys School. Mr. Ford designed the ventilation system personally.

(Illustration by E. Laurie Loftus)

The Indian Communal Grinding Stone

Located in an abandoned park near the junction of Green Hill Road and Singletary Lane in South Sudbury, the Communal Indian grinding stone bears mute witness to a time when Green and Goodman's hills were the site of a large summer encampment of Nipmucs or Nipnets dating back well before the 16th Century.

The stone is an erratic boulder some six feet in diameter standing a little more than three feet high. Its top surface is broken by a broad shallow basin, the grinding bowl, where generations of Indian women and maids ground acorns and maize into meal. A shallow shelf on the downhill side of the stone may have been used by warriors standing watch against possible intruders.

Back in the '50s, the stone was authenticated by Dr. Hallam Leonard Movius, Associate Professor in the Department of Anthropology at Harvard University and later by Benjamin Lincoln Smith, then director of the Massachusetts Historical Society.

Smith noted that the absence of moss and lichen in the bowl of the stone authenticates its use for grinding grain. He believed that the rock absorbed oils from the grain over years of use and this oil discouraged any fungus growth.

It was near this spot that a delegation of white men from Watertown first met Karte, the Nipmuc chieftain whom they later called Goodman. (Illustration by Donald M. Starr)

The '50s

Houses and Schools and Taxes, Oh My!

Suddenly the growth that appeared to be but a post-war novelty in the '40s began mushrooming through the town like a cancer out of control. The town quickly learned that the rudimentary zoning regulations it had passed in the '30s were no match for well-heeled and savvy developers, but it would be nearly five years before more stringent laws were enacted.

The signs were everywhere. The town petitioned the federal government for a new post office that would consolidate the services of the South Sudbury, Sudbury Center and North Sudbury offices. Edward Hill, then owner of Hilco Supply, and Les Hall both offered building sites. Hill's location next to the Goodnow Library and the Sudbury Shopping Center (now MacKinnon's) was judged to be more central. The new office, with Forrest Bradshaw as Postmaster, was opened in 1953.

By 1955, Sudbury was listed among the ten fastest-growing towns with populations under 10,000 in Massachusetts, and Building Inspector/Fire Chief Al St. Germain complained that he had twice as much work as the year before and was forced to do inspections on Saturdays and Sundays in order to keep up.

The population had reached 4,000 by 1955 and the schools were feeling the pinch. A Permanent School Building Committee, chaired by Ed Krietsek, was appointed to see to the feasibility and construction of one or more district elementary schools. By the end of the decade, four had been constructed, along with the Ephraim Curtis Junior High off Pratt's Mill Road and the Lincoln-Sudbury Regional High School.

In the meantime, students were stuffed into such offbeat places as the Boston Edison building (now dismantled) near today's Buddy Dog Humane Society, the two-room South School on Massasoit Avenue, and the Peter Noyes School gymnasium.

With 840 kids in the school system and teachers drawing between $3,400 and $3,700 annually, there wasn't much left in the town budget and other departments were forced to skimp. The folly of this became apparent on December 22, 1955 when the Wayside Inn was nearly destroyed by fire. Sudbury's newest piece of fire apparatus was a 1943 Ford pumper given to the town by Henry Ford.

Mutual Aid from six neighboring communities knocked down the fire before the building was a total loss, but there followed nearly three months of anxious waiting before the town received word that the Ford Foundation would foot the $700,000 bill for restoring the ancient hostelry.

The first volleys of a battle that would last for more than fifteen years sounded early in the decade when the Boston Edison Company announced it would run high-tension transmission lines across the Sudbury marshes. It wasn't until 1966 that Edison capitulated and re-routed the lines.

By the second half of the decade, Sudbury voters found themselves at a crossroads. Either the tax base had to be expanded or the town--particularly the school department--would have to tighten its belt severely. Abel Cutting and Joseph Brown were named to an Industrial Development Board to attract "clean" industry to Sudbury. Among the companies eventually recruited were Raytheon Corporation and Sperry Rand.

And as the decade ended, another controversy loomed. An article on the Water District warrant, calling for the addition of fluoride to the town water supply in order to reduce dental cavities in the town's youth, drew fire from Christian Scientists and others who felt their individual rights were being violated.

And along the way there were the little things. Gus Sharkey's Saturday night dances at the Town Hall attracted an average of 100 townspeople and paid for themselves. The band, with Dave Bentley on the trumpet, later became known as the Suburbanaires.

In 1951 the Boston and Maine Railroad announced that the old depot and stationmaster would be replaced by an automatic signal and a smaller building. Superintendent of Schools Owen B. Kiernan announced his retirement and decried the rapidly rising school enrollment brought on by the "Baby Bubble."

Selectman Harvey Fairbank made a pitch for home rule in the 1952 Town Report, noting that: "At times we wonder if more good might not be done for cities and towns if the lawmaking bodies of the state and federal governments were to vote to take laws off the books rather than put more on."

Later, Fairbank couldn't resist tooting the horn for town government, saying: "It is our candid opinion that the people of Sudbury and those from without who have business with our departments have the good fortune to receive more and better service than is received in other towns of our size. We realize that there are unhappy situations at times, but, as a whole, very satisfactory service is rendered by your public servants."

Town employees did a lot for a little in the '50s. Combined salaries and expenses, with the exception of the schools, amounted to only $36,500 in 1952 while the welfare and charity bill was $34,000. The school budget amounted to $128,000, a sum that the Finance Committee "recommended under protest."

Herbert J. and Esther M. Atkinson, owners of the Sudbury Laboratories, formed the Sudbury Foundation in 1952, and by 1955, had assets of $39,542.53. That figure increased to $45,911.40 in 1956.

Complaints on the appearance and haphazard development of the Boston Post Road in 1957 prompted the Selectmen to suggest more stringent zoning by-laws, but the horse was already out of the barn by then. The Planning Board conducted a survey and discovered something that is still true today: "Despite high taxes, there is little sentiment for economy. Apparently few of our people are hurting."

In 1958, the Welfare Board complained that nursing home rates had increased from $5.50 to $6.50 a day. The Town's real estate valuation increased by $3,325,690 to $9,017,355 in a single year. The tax rate rose to $81.50 per thousand.

In 1959, architect Ralph Adams Cramm deeded seven acres of his estate on Concord Road, including St. Elizabeth's Chapel, to St. Elizabeth's Church. A complete set of plans for a new church building at the corner of Concord and Morse Roads was part of the deal.

Down the road, the old Featherland Farm property was purchased by a holding company of private citizens and then turned over to the town for use as a public recreation area. It's known as Featherland Park today.

And in the town center a landmark took one step closer to becoming town property. Florence Armes Hosmer, whose family had lived beside the common since 1897, signed an agreement turning the Hosmer House over to the town when she died. In return, the town allowed her to live in the building tax-free for the remainder of her life. She died in 1978, aged 97.

The Committee on Town Administration ran a study of the Town's growth, taxes and debts and came up with some predictions that were a tad off the mark. It predicted that school enrollment would be 2,128 in 1964 (it was 2,485) and that the tax rate would rise to $114 per thousand (by dint of some penny pinching it was $102). The committee predicted a real estate valuation in 1964 of $20 million. The actual figure was $22,213,225.

And the growth wasn't stopping. A record 326 building permits were issued in 1959.

XVIII

Let's Buy a Little Place in Sudbury

The zoning by-laws approved by the Annual Town Meeting of March 6, 1939, were pretty simple: minimum of 20,000 square feet, 50 foot setback in front, 20 on the sides and 30 in back. No building could occupy more than 40 percent of the area of the lot and God help you if you raised pigs, chickens or mink in the backyard without a permit.

This worked well when there were only 669 dwelling houses in town which were taxed at a rate of $29 per thousand, and the entire school enrollment from first grade through high school was only 357. By 1950, there were 845 dwellings, 493 children in the school system and the tax rate had exactly doubled. To make matters worse, developers were buying up large tracts of land all over town, carving them up into half-acre lots, and selling them to young couples seeking a bucolic life in what was beginning to be fashionably known as "The Suburbs."

And the suburbs were popular. Permanent Building Committee Chairman Ed Kreitsek determined that in the decade between 1954 and 1964 the town quadrupled in size, more growth than in any decade since 1775. Route 128 was completed and soon industries that had been located in the city moved west to cheaper locations. This move put them within commuting distance of Sudbury.

Something else was happening as well. Sudbury's small farmers could no longer hire help for room and board and $35 a week. Men and women returning from the armed forces were highly trained and found a ready job market for their talents. Growing corn or beans in Sudbury's rocky soil was no longer a profitable venture and many landowners were only too happy to sell out to developers.

"Nobody was building out here, it was all farms," recalled builder Walter Beckett who started developing the old Warren

Hunt farm at the corner of Concord and Old Lancaster roads in 1954. "There were blackberry bushes as high as your head. It was a regular jungle." [1]

While Sudbury's zoning laws were lax, they were more stringent than in surrounding towns, and, consequently, young married couples would buy smaller houses in Framingham or Maynard and move to Sudbury later when they had children and could afford a more expensive home.

It was not long before the handwriting began to appear on the wall. In October 1954, Highway Superintendent Alvin Noyes warned: "Developments during the past year or two seem to indicate that, unless there is a sudden change in the trend, Sudbury is about to evolve quite suddenly from a small country town to a congested residential suburb."

By 1955, Fire Chief/Building Inspector Albert St. Germain noted that his workload had doubled and Saturday and Sunday inspections were necessary in order to keep abreast. In 1955, 207 dwellings, one school, 11 business buildings, and 28 alterations and additions had been constructed.

Town Meeting took the hesitant first steps toward alleviating the situation in 1953 by establishing three different single-residence housing zones with minimum lot sizes and frontages for each. Zone A (once the entire town) was raised from 20,000 square feet to 22,000 square feet with 150-foot frontage. Lots in Zone B had a 40,000 minimum and those in Zone C, 60,000. The article also provided that all lots laid out prior to the passing of the by-law would be grandfathered, providing they met with all setback requirements and had a house built on them within five years.

But the effort was too little too late. Two hundred and sixty-six building permits were issued in 1955 and the real estate valuation rose above $4 million for the first time. The Finance Committee noted that salaries of town employees needed adjusting, but that there was no money. The Committee recommended $537,450, most of it for schools. It amounted to an increase of $113,708 over the previous year's appropriation.

Town Meeting addressed the lot size problem again at a Special Session on June 25, 1955, enlarging lots in Zone A to 30,000 square feet and keeping the minimums in Zones B and C as they were.

Still, the Town appeared to be falling apart at the seams. Another new school was needed, road construction and repair was way behind schedule and many town departments, including Police and Fire, were woefully short of manpower and up-to-date equipment. [2]

"The town has been in the headlines as one of the ten fastest growing towns in the state with populations under 10,000," reported Selectman Harvey Fairbank. "The population of about 4,000 is about double what it was ten years ago [in 1945]. The amount of the tax bill is of much more concern than the tax rate or the assessment and this is controlled entirely by the amount of money that is voted at town meetings.

"Many of the new people in Sudbury come from places where they were too far removed from public officials and the wheels of government to have any immediate influence, in all probability. It should not be difficult here for everyone interested to have their influence felt."

Unfortunately, the newcomers to Sudbury were already having their influence felt, but not in the way that Fairbank had intended. Developer Alfred Halper's Wayside Acres subdivision in the Pratt's Mill Road area won six national awards for excellence. When one of his split-level creations was featured on the cover of *Better Homes and Gardens Magazine*, inquiries flooded in from all over the country.

When some citizens in town tried to tie increased taxes and town expenses to his coat tails, Halper responded with a letter to the editor of the *Sudbury Citizen* saying that he helped young residents by "building the kind of house people want at a price they can pay."

In 1958, the developers successfully fought back zoning changes that would have increased the lot size in Zones B and

C to 60,000 and 80,000 square feet respectively. Town meeting did approve raising the minimum size of lots in Zone A to 40,000 square feet. Later an amendment was added grandfathering all lots laid out before the passage of the article at 30,000 square feet.

As more and more young families with children were attracted to Sudbury, the demand for more schools and town services increased, and taxes rose right with them. It wasn't long before wiser heads started thinking of ways to spread the tax burden. The answer was obvious: industry.

In November 1952, Abel Cutting, who would later chair the Industrial Development Commission for the town, bought a page in the program for the senior class play and ran what the School Department considered a controversial advertisement. It depicted a gravestone upon which was carved: "Here lies Sudbury, without industry." The school administration required that each copy be stamped with the message that it was not authorized by the School Committee or administration. The following year a similar ad appeared.

It would be four years before Cutting's effort began to bear fruit, but by the end of the decade, both Raytheon Corporation and Sperry Rand had built research and development facilities in town.

Sudbury's troubles were still far from over. While the influx of business and industry would bring some tax relief down the road, the Town needed new schools right now. The burgeoning 1954 school enrollment of 761 children was jammed into the Center School and Peter Noyes School buildings with the spillover at the South School and a building on Route 20 rented from the Boston Edison Company.

The first step came at the 1954 Town Meeting where Sudbury voters appropriated $15,000 for the use of a Regional School Planning Committee and later, in a Special Town Meeting the following December, unanimously approved a $1,400,000 bond issue for construction of the Lincoln-Sudbury Regional High School. The new Regional School opened September 10, 1956, with 22 teachers and 247 students, 185 of them from Sudbury.

In 1955, the Town Meeting voted to appoint "a Low Cost School Housing Committee to determine the advisability and feasibility of erecting one or more district elementary schools in the town. And particularly to look into locating available sites for such schools as well as the feasibility or advisability of adding to the present elementary school of the town at a construction and equipment cost of no more than $700 per pupil. Said Committee to consist of one member of the School Committee, one member of the Planning Board, one member of the Finance Committee and two citizens appointed by the moderator."

The Committee did its work well and quickly. Over the summer it acquired options on three sites and presented its findings to the Town at a November 5 Special Town Meeting.

Town Meeting tabled plans to purchase with entailments a 10-acre plot of land from the Cutler family for a district school. [4] While not unwilling sellers, the Cutlers preferred that the town continue to search in the area. The voters did appropriate $5,000 for eight acres of land on Horse Pond Road and $13,750 for a nine-and-one-half acre plot on Haynes Road. The sum of $8,400 was appropriated for 10 acres of Cutler land on Woodside Road a year later (with entailments that would allow land to revert to the Cutlers if it ceased being used for a school within a 20-year time period.)

The following year the town appropriated $450,000 for construction and equipment of a new school at the Horse Pond Road site. The new building came in $15,000 under budget and was occupied by 120 pupils on March 14, 1958, drawing raves for its utilitarian design which included a cafeteria with tables and benches that folded into the walls to create an auditorium or play area.

Completion of Horse Pond took off some of the pressure, allowing the School Committee to discontinue use of the Edison Building on the Post Road and the Lincoln-South building in Lincoln which was provided as a courtesy until Lincoln-Sudbury was completed, but Sudbury wasn't out of the woods yet. The committee predicted that more new elementary schools would be needed soon.

While construction was going on, the School Committee was taking steps to assure that Sudbury children would be taught by the best teachers available. A revised salary schedule for teachers was adopted which provided minimum salaries from $3,400 to $3,700. These were quickly increased to $3,800 for a B.S. and $4,000 for a master's degree. In 1955, 41 teachers were supervising the education of 840 kids. [5]

The assessed real estate valuation rose to $5,691,665 in 1957, the first time over $5 million. The tax rate rose to $81.50, an increase of $9.50 in a single year. Some 1,533 dwellings were assessed, up 378 from 1956. These numbers really began to sink in when parents discovered that their children were once more in crowded classrooms or in temporary quarters at the Peter Noyes school gymnasium.

At the Town Meeting of March 6, 1957 the Town girded for the inevitable. The Low Cost School Building Committee was reincarnated as the Permanent School Building Committee and charged with making surveys at the Haynes, Loring and Fairbank School sites and then overseeing bids and construction as directed by the School Committee and the Town. One of its first moves was the purchase of land for the Fairbank Road School for $14,000.

"It was a sensible thing to do," said Ed Kreitsek, who served on the Committee from 1955 to 1962. "There were lots of things to do. When the need for another school came along, Town Meeting might have had to find five other guys, [for the building committee] and then after that, five other guys, all of whom would have to learn the process.

"Getting state aid requires a lot of complicated paper work, but we knew how to do it and get a fairly quick response. So I suggested we change the name from Low Cost School Building Committee to Permanent Building Committee so we could continue to use the same know-how for other schools."

The original Committee was chaired by real estate man Don Neelon and included Kreitsek, Stephen E. Grande Jr., Robert J. Caldwell and Francis G. Publicover. By the time it had disbanded in 1962, it had supervised the construction of seven schools, two fire stations and a police station.

Horse Pond School was not even occupied before the Committee went to work getting the Fairbank Road project off the ground. An unprecedented budget hearing was hosted by the Finance Committee to discuss articles at an upcoming Town Meeting pertaining to schools. A record 300 citizens showed up, attracted by the opportunity to tour the soon-to-be-opened Horse Pond Road facility.

They were told that the Special Town Meeting would be asked to appropriate $450,000 to speed the construction at Fairbank. On February 6 the voters did them one better, approving $485,000 for the new facility by a 253-10 margin. [6]

Construction had hardly begun before newly-appointed Superintendent-Principal C. Newton Heath, noting that first through fifth graders at Horse Pond School were on double sessions awaiting the completion of Fairbank school, predicted the need for another new elementary school and a new junior high by 1961. "We can't stop Sudbury from growing," editorialized the *Sudbury Citizen*. All we can do is grow with it and provide for the educational needs of our children."

The Town apparently agreed. On October 21, 1958, a Special Town Meeting voted 134-12 to appropriate $1,005,000 for TWO new elementary schools, one on Woodside Road in East Sudbury and the other to be built on land located off Old Lancaster Road to be taken by eminent domain. Later the site was changed to land off Concord Road and became the Nixon School.

Indeed, 1958 was a record year for enrollment in Sudbury schools. Four hundred fifty-three students registered at Lincoln-Sudbury, and 1,172 in elementary and junior high, as residents flooded the local newspapers with letters urging more zoning controls to lessen the financial pressure caused by the influx of school-age children.

More than 200 voters showed up at Finance Committee meetings in early October and got some more shocking news. The elementary schools needed $1,050,000; more land needed to be purchased for schools over and above the $1,050,000 earmarked for Loring and Nixon, and $4,500 was needed for an engineering study at the High School. The school population was exploding, and the tax rate, at $85 per thousand, was exploding right with it.

As the decade came to a close, the emphasis shifted from building elementary schools to reining in what many considered to be extravagant and excessive per-pupil costs at Lincoln Sudbury. Administrators defended the $562.95 per year expense for educating each child at L-S. Critics pointed out that Weston, at $649.64, was the only high school spending more.

There was also the matter of a $20,000 appropriation for plans to build a $1,275,000 addition onto the high school that raised the voters' hackles. A hearing was scheduled the month prior to Town Meeting and the *Sudbury Citizen* editorialized that voters should focus on quality of teaching and scholarship standing, not just numbers. The planning money request passed, and, later at a Special Town Meeting, the bond issue--less $275,000 for a proposed auditorium--was approved as well. That, along with an additional $275,000 for schools, pushed the tax rate up an additional $5 to $90.

With Raytheon and Sperry Rand soon to be pumping tax money into the Town's coffers and four schools in various stages of construction, Sudbury taxpayers headed into the '60s enjoying a slight respite. But there would be more headaches ahead.

XIX

"The Wayside Inn is Burning Down!"

Curt Harding and Jeanne Fredey were high school sweethearts and two of the most popular members of the Sudbury High School Class of 1953, so it was no surprise that the guest list for their wedding at Newton's Grace Episcopal Church on the evening of December 21, 1955, was a Who's Who of old Sudbury families. Guy Palmer, one of Curt's old basketball teammates, was best man and David Hawes, son of Moderator L. Roy "Tim" Hawes of North Sudbury, was one of the ushers. [1]

The list was so extensive that Jean Fredey, the father of the bride, took the precaution of booking the spacious north ballroom at the Wayside Inn for the wedding reception. Among the guests dining and dancing before the roaring fire in the great north fireplace were Eleanor and Jim Greenawalt.

Greenawalt had recently been named a captain by newly-appointed fire chief Albert St. Germain, partly because of his firefighting skills and partly because he lived conveniently close to the fire station. His wife, the former Eleanor Goulding, was right at home in the Inn, having attended the Southwest School and taken dancing lessons in the same low-ceilinged ballroom.

Outside in the parking lot, cars started hard as the last guests headed homeward at 11:30 p.m. New England had been in the grip of a severe cold snap for the better part of a week and meteorologist E. B. Rideout predicted that it would continue for some days more. The temperature was already zero and falling fast. Since it was a Tuesday night, there were no overnight guests at the Inn.

Night Watchman William Mann of Marlborough clocked in at midnight, made his first set of rounds and set about cleaning up the mess in the north ballroom. The job still wasn't finished when it was time for his second round at 2 a.m. On the lower floor near one of the pantries he smelled something unusual. Opening the door to the boiler room, he was greeted by a puff of smoke.

Mann slammed the door and retreated to the registration desk in the old bar room where he phoned Assistant Inn Director George Griffin who was asleep in the coach house across the street. It took several rings before Griffin awakened. He instructed Mann to notify Innkeeper John Saint at his home on the Boston Post Road, hung up, and dialed the fire department.

Meanwhile, others had become aware that something was amiss at the Inn. A trailer truck driver on the Route 20 bypass smelled smoke and saw flames shooting from the windows of the north wing. He flagged down a Marlborough police cruiser and passed on the information, but by the time it had been relayed to Sudbury, the alarm had already been given. At the same time, Inn hostess Priscilla Staples was awakened by a bright light shining in her bedroom window. Looking out, she saw the entire north wing in flames.

Leo Quinn, the town's only permanent firefighter besides Chief St. Germain, glanced at the clock as he fumbled for the telephone on his bedside table at the Loring Parsonage. It read 2:20 a.m. He put out the call over the monitors in the homes of the town's 20 call firefighters, crossed the driveway to the fire station, and cranked up Engine Four, a '43 Ford pumper given the town by the Wayside Inn. This truck, equipped for high-pressure fog, and carrying 500 gallons of water, was the nearest thing to a piece of Class A fire apparatus that the town owned.

The call box awakened St. Germain from a sound sleep at his home on Peakham Road, a ten-minute drive from the Inn. He turned on the two-way radio in his cruiser and immediately received a call from Police Sergeant Ernest Ryan who was already on the scene.

"It's bad," said Ryan. "I'd send for as much mutual aid as you can get." St. Germain immediately radioed a second alarm that brought units from Framingham, Marlborough, Southborough, Wayland, Weston and Concord to the scene.

Quinn raced Engine Four down the service road to the rear of the Inn and pulled up as close to the building as the heat would allow. Flames were already shooting from the serving room windows on the second story of the north wing and the roar of the fire could be heard from a great distance. Mickey Hriniak, a call firefighter with only one arm, helped Quinn pull booster lines from the truck but the fire was too hot and the water did no good.

By the time St. Germain arrived on the scene at 2:35 a.m. the second floor of the north wing was totally engulfed in flames and the fire was beginning to work its way back toward the kitchens below. As the Chief radioed for more mutual aid, Captain Greenawalt, who left the building only hours before, arrived with Engine Three, a 1942 International that carried 500 gallons of water.

Grabbing fire axes from the trucks, St. Germain and Greenawalt started chopping a hole in the ice on Josephine Pond, a small impoundment to the rear of the Inn that services the ice house. The ice was 16 inches thick and it took the men nearly ten minutes before they had a hole large enough to take the intake hoses from the two pumpers. The International and a pumper from Marlborough set in and started pumping water to supply other trucks as they arrived.

By 2:45 a.m., eleven pieces of apparatus were on the scene, two each from Framingham, Marlborough and Wayland and a ladder truck from Concord. Several attempted to draw water from Hop Brook to the west of the Inn, but wound up sucking air. The nearest fire hydrant was more than a mile to the east at Ecke's Motel.

By 3 a.m. nearly 100 firefighters were pouring thousands of gallons of water from 20 hose lines on the inferno, but the fire continued to make headway. Flames spread to the West Wing which contained the 1800 ballroom and the tap room, and started to work horizontally toward the older rooms in the front of the building, which were filled with priceless antiques. St. Germain ordered two engines from Framingham to concentrate on cutting the fire off in the East Wing and they succeeded in stopping the flames at the old kitchen. The display pewter on the tables was melted by the intense heat and the wainscoting and ceiling planks scorched, but a thick coating of ice preserved most of the furniture.

Elsewhere, things weren't going as well. The 16-below-zero temperatures slushed up the water in the pumps of the two big engines drawing water from the pond and gasoline heaters had to be rushed in to get them going again. A gauge froze up on a Wayland pumper, increasing the pressure in an inch and one half handline to more than 1,000 pounds. Two Wayland firefighters were sent sprawling and Robert Groton was transported to Leonard Morse Hospital in Natick with a broken leg.

As the night wore on, the trucks began to run short of fuel and Algy Alexander and the Interstate Oil Company were asked to open their stations and relay gas and oil to the site to keep them going. By the time the final all out was broadcast, 200 gallons of fuel had been consumed.

There was a touch of humor amid the tragedy. Nobscot Boy Scout Reservation ranger Freddie Craig, a call firefighter, reached into the icy waters of Josephine Pond to clear a hose strainer and came up with a handful of one very surprised horned pout!

Meanwhile the word had spread throughout the town. The Sudbury Civil Defense, Red Cross and Grange set up a canteen at the Town Hall and started relaying coffee and sandwiches to the firefighters at the Inn. There they were distributed by Mrs. Alfred Gardner and Mrs. Thomas Cahill. Paul Ecke, owner of Ecke's Motel, appeared with a huge Thermos of hot Irish coffee.

By 3:30 a.m. the fire was under control in the East Wing but flames broke through the gambrel roof on the main house and the fire vented itself out. Police Chief John McGovern was on the spot with his cameras as firefighters forced the front door, only to be greeted by a flash of flame and smoke. His dramatic picture was picked up by the Associated Press News Service and carried on the front page of newspapers all over the globe.

Several volunteers rushed into the front rooms of the Inn to see if anything could be salvaged, but Jerusha Howe's pianoforte and the "Somber Clock" that Longfellow immortalized were frozen to the floor and covered by a thick coating of ice. Small items, such as the Molineaux etchings and Howe coat of arms, were covered with thick layers of soot, but survived. Two priceless Paul Revere prints were a total loss and the Howe family bible and its box were badly scorched. Water pouring down the front staircase quickly froze into a glistening cascade. Outside, the firefighters were barely recognizable, their helmets, heavy slickers and boots coated with layers of ice.

By 4 a.m. the North and West Wings were totally demolished and the firefighters concentrated their efforts on the front of the building. St. Germain declared the building a "total loss" and later set damages at $200,000, not counting the many priceless antiques. By the time the blaze was brought under control, a million gallons of water--four times the capacity of the town's storage tank on Goodman's Hill--had been pumped on the remains of the Inn. Under the ice of Josephine Pond, all that remained was mud.

By dawn the word had spread far and wide. The Inn fire made the front pages as far away as the *New York Times* and was carried on all the wire services.

The fire was out, but immediately a new question arose. Would the Inn be rebuilt and continue its tradition of hospitality? Or would it go the way of many other old buildings that had burned and just become an historic site, devoid of life and charm? There was but one acceptable answer to that question and the citizens of Sudbury immediately took steps to see that it would be the right one.

Less than six hours after the last engine returned to quarters, the Sudbury Board of Selectmen met in emergency session and voted unanimously to offer the Ford Foundation "any cooperation and community effort deemed necessary," to rebuild the Inn.

The following day, groups from all over the community were

meeting. Twenty Wayside Inn abutters met at the home of Robert Caldwell on Peakham Road, which, only a few years before, had been Henry Ford's Southwest Schoolhouse; Don Atkins called an emergency meeting of the Sudbury-Wayland Kiwanis Club and the Reverend Ernest Bodenweber of the Memorial Congregational Church hosted a meeting of the Sudbury clergy.

Out of these meetings came the formation of the Citizens Committee for the Preservation of the Wayside Inn, with Boston Banker Edmund Sears and attorney John C. Powers, as vice chairmen and Calvin Smith and insurance man Leslie Hall, the Sudbury Town Historian, as prime movers.

The committee knew there could be no delay. Ford Vice President of Public Relations Charles F. Moore was planning a fact-finding trip to Sudbury in early January, accompanied by experts from the Ford Foundation and the Ford Motor Company. It was important that the Ford delegation realize how much the Inn meant to Sudbury and its neighbors. A massive letter-writing campaign was the only answer.

Powers took a month off from his law practice to coordinate the effort. With the help of his father, a columnist at the *Boston Globe*, he launched a publicity campaign that kept the Inn's plight in the headlines. Soon offers of antique furniture, old paneling, period fireplaces and even a cage of live finches started pouring in from all over the country.

More than 40,000 brochures explaining the Inn's plight and including a quote from Henry Ford: "Nothing that is good ever dies," were printed and sent to public officials, private citizens and civic groups all over the country. The Sudbury High School Student Council sent a check to cover part of the $1,000 postage bill and members of the committee, now headed by Al Gardner, the president of the Boston Bar Association, dug into their pockets to come up with the rest.

High school students volunteered to stamp and address chain letters, businessmen on cross-country trips dropped off brochures wherever they went and politicians sought support from people in power at all levels of the government.

"Our pitch was to kill them with kindness," Powers recalled later. "We just wanted to say thanks for keeping the Inn going so long. It was an enormous event and there were so many people in town who helped us out."

The efforts paid off in spades. By the time Moore and his delegation arrived in Sudbury January 4, 1956, more than 10,000 letters had arrived at either Sudbury or Dearborn, Michigan, and more were on their way at the rate of a boxcar full a day. They included appeals from Presidents Harry S. Truman and Herbert Hoover, Senator John F. Kennedy, former House Speaker Joe Martin and Supreme Court Justice Felix Frankfurter.

Townspeople hoping for a quick decision from the Ford interests were disappointed. Moore stated that meetings with the Citizens Committee were beneficial, but it would be at least two weeks, and probably a month, before a decision could be made.

"We don't want to just erect another building," he told the *Boston Traveler*. "Our decision will be based on cost, the ability to obtain materials, and whether the experts feel that there is enough left of the building upon which to start. My personal impression is that enough of the building and materials remain to justify a restoration job."

Unbeknownst to the Citizen's Committee, Moore had more than his personal observations to go on. The day after the fire, Dr. Donald A. Shelly, Director of the Henry Ford Museum at Greenfield Village in Dearborn, had sent Roy Woodbury Baker, the Chief Custodian for the Society for the Preservation of New England Antiquities, to see if the Inn was worth restoring. Baker not only said that it was, but told Shelly he'd be very interested in supervising the job.

Meanwhile, local residents were hedging their bets. Representative James DeNormandie of Lincoln introduced a resolution in the Massachusetts House of Representatives calling for the restoration of the Wayside Inn. It was approved on January 6.

The rest of January dragged on with no word from Dearborn and nerves all over Sudbury were fraying. On February 12, the *Boston Herald* carried the page one headline "Sudbury Ready to Restore Wayside Inn if Fords Don't." The Citizens Committee stood ready to call on thousands of offers of assistance from all over the world if the Fords failed to come through.

Six days later, their wait was over. On February 18, William Clay Ford, President of the Wayside Inn Board of Trustees, delivered the good news: "I am delighted to report that the Ford Foundation, through its president Mr.H. Rowan Gaither, Jr., has informed me that the Foundation will undertake financial responsibility for the restoration of the Wayside Inn."

On February 23, 1956, Gaither made it official with the announcement that the Foundation would supply $500,000 for the restoration work. Just two months and two days after the fire--64 days that seemed more like an eternity--the *Sudbury Citizen* carried the news in a banner headline across its front page: "Wayside Inn to Live Again."

Henry Ford's words were prophetic. "Nothing that is good ever dies."

Chief Albert St. Germain's Fire Department report in the 1955 *Town Report* made no mention of the Wayside Inn fire, but did recommend the purchase of a Class A pumper with a tank capacity of at least 750 gallons. "I sincerely hope that the citizens of Sudbury will insist on the purchase of a real fire truck this time," he commented.

Town Meeting did just that. The following March, $8,000 was appropriated for a new Class A pumper. Sudbury would not get caught short again.

XX
A Question of Individual Rights

The annual meeting of the Sudbury Water District had traditionally been an open and shut affair with the biggest question on the agenda whether or not a quorum was present. Once enough people were in the hall, the questions of extending water mains, setting rates and purchasing new equipment were settled with dispatch and everyone was well on the way home by 9 p.m.

But that was before some well-meaning soul suggested that the District add fluoride to the town water. That little article on the 1959 Water District warrant would turn the town upside down for more than a year.

On the surface it sounded like a pretty good idea. After all, there were a ton of kids in town, and leading nutritionists, including Sudbury's own Dr. Jean Mayer, touted fluoride's benefits in preventing tooth decay. This was a win-win situation. The expense was minimal compared to the projected savings in dental bills. Anybody who opposed this had to be "a quack or a religious fanatic" according to one proponent. [1]

Quacks and fanatics were in short supply, but Christian Scientists and individual rights advocates were not. When a trial balloon letter to the editor of the *Sudbury Citizen* supporting fluoridation surfaced, they blasted it as a violation of individual rights and cited independent surveys that indicated fluoride's role in preventing tooth decay was over-rated. [2]

"No-one forces their way into our kitchen and demands that we eat only a certain kind of food of which they approve, or not eat at all," wrote a Sudbury mother of two. "This is a scare campaign," countered a proponent. "The writer should contact the American Dental Association."

As the date of the Annual Water District Meeting drew closer, the town divided into opposing camps. The Fluoridationists, led by Mayer, W. L. Pritchard and R. S. Holway, pointed out that fluoride wasn't a medicine, but a foodstuff related to salt, and cited overwhelming scientific evidence that fluoride was beneficial in the prevention of tooth decay.

"Well-meaning people concerned quite properly with basic issues such as personal liberty, public safety and socialization find themselves allied with those who oppose fluoridation on religious grounds," they said, intimating that this should not happen.

The 200 members of the Citizens Committee Against Fluoridation, led by Buzz Kane, Carlton Ellms and Elizabeth Atkinson, circulated a petition opposing fluoridation on individual rights grounds. "There is no efficient way to fluoridate water individually," they pointed out. Citizens shouldn't be forced to dig their own wells or buy bottled water because of the will of the majority.

The proponents took a new tack. They set up all the arguments against fluoridation like so many birds on a fence and attempted to shoot them down, one by one.

"The arguments against fluoridation are varied and productive but they all reduce to several major themes," they said. "Fluoride is a poison; Fluoride is mass medicine and socialized medicine; Fluoride corrodes pipes and equipment (this proved to be true) and is dangerous; Fluoride use is a violation of constitutionally-guaranteed personal liberties; Fluoride use should be handled individually rather than publicly.

"There is no appreciable opposition to the thesis that fluoride is beneficial in preventing tooth decay," they went on. "There is overwhelming evidence from a Canadian independent study; Fluoride is not a medicine, but a foodstuff related to salt; There is no way to fluoridate water individually." [3]

Then things got nasty. "Those who oppose fluoridation are against children," sniffed one proponent. "All those who oppose artificial fluoridation are either religious crackpots or quacks."

"People knowing both sides of the question want no part of fluoridation," countered the opposition "Fluoride's safety has never been proven; costs of the program are grossly underestimated; Fluoride's acceptance is highly exaggerated. And," they added, "Every individual under our laws has the right to say what shall be done with his or her body. No other supporting evidence is necessary."

The matter came to a head on February 23, 1959, when 142 voters jammed the Peter Noyes gym-auditorium. Debate was quickly cut off and the fluoridation concept was approved 89-53. There was a mad rush for the door following the vote and the remaining articles on the warrant could not be considered for lack of a quorum. Among them was an article approving funds for the purchase of fluoridation equipment. [4] Suddenly, the District found itself with an authorization to use fluoride, but no equipment with which to carry it out. It was the first adjournment for lack of a quorum in the history of the Water District.

The battle was far from over. The Water Commissioners' request for equipment funds at a District meeting on May 7 was denied by a 108-96 secret ballot vote. A Special District Meeting was called for November 6 to appropriate money for equipment. Everyone settled in for a long, hot summer. [5]

The fur flew thick and fast with both sides bringing in experts to support their point of view, but the rhetoric, while it attracted more people to the fray, did little to change the outcome. This time the appropriation for equipment was approved by a 178-153 secret ballot vote.

Fluoridation equipment was finally installed at Sudbury's three pumping stations just three months later. The controversy was over, but the feelings it aroused lasted for a long, long time and there are still people in town who wonder "Did we do the right thing?"

XXI

The Power Line Fight

History has a way of repeating itself and Sudbury is certainly no exception, but it is ironic that one of the Town's biggest battles of the 20th Century took place over the same piece of ground that the Town's founders defended against King Philip's Indian forces in 1676.

There were no casualties in this skirmish, unless you take into account the pocketbooks of the taxpayers and the Boston Edison Company. The fight went on for nine years before the power company finally got the message that the citizens of Sudbury were not about to give up and go away.

Just what was at issue depends on which side you talk to. To Edison, it was a simple matter of building seven miles of high voltage transmission line through the Sudbury River marshes from Wayland through Sudbury and Concord to Acton. To Sudbury, it was a question of self-determination and home rule, or, as many people put it, not getting pushed around.

Edison went about its business the way it always had in the past. After all, it was the town's biggest taxpayer and--as Town Clerk Lawrence Tighe dutifully pointed out--always the first to pay. The proposal for the new line was announced on May 26, 1960, and a Department of Public Utilities (DPU) hearing was set for the morning of June 21.

If Edison's executives thought that approval of the new lines was nothing more than a formality, they would change their minds in a hurry. Despite the morning hour 80 citizens attended the hearing and voiced unanimous opposition. The DPU Commissioners promised to render a decision in six weeks, and, in fact, did so on August 18, 1960. "Beauty doesn't count," they said. "The line is necessary."

But Sudbury didn't agree. Two hundred fifty residents signed on for a campaign to oppose the Edison lines. They pointed out that the "H"-shaped wooden towers would destroy the Haynes Garrison House site on Water Row as well as Harry Rice's farm and airport and an Indian burial ground

At a jam-packed Special Town Meeting that September, voters authorized the Board of Selectmen to oppose the power lines and appropriated $5,000 for the town counsel to do so. A Power and Light Committee was appointed to direct the opposition. It was well after midnight before the meeting broke up and for hours after that townspeople gathered in small groups outside the Hall discussing the situation.

They pointed out that the 150-acre Harry Rice property along the river meadows was among the most scenic in the area and harbored an airstrip, a Civil Air Patrol facility, a riding stable and the town dog pound. It was also noted that Rice, while digging a new cesspool, had discovered the burial site of a Red Paint Indian woman surrounded by a large collection of artifacts.

Meanwhile, negotiations with Edison were getting nowhere. A Sudbury Citizens Committee offered a tax abatement if the lines were put underground. "Too expensive" ($517,000 overhead as against $975,000 underground), Edison replied. Special Counsel Philip B. Buzzell noted that Edison might need permission from Governor Frank Sargeant and the Governor's Council to run lines anywhere through the Pantry Brook Wildlife Management Area. "Only bird watchers care about power lines," Edison countered.

In January 1962, things began to come to a head. Edison lawyers obtained a ruling from the Massachusetts Supreme Court allowing the land for the power line to be taken by eminent domain. The following August, the company informed the Sudbury Selectmen that it intended to do so.

Another morning hearing was scheduled for September 20, 1962, at 10 a.m. Edison showed up with plot plans, maps and charts. More than 100 citizens sat silently and listened. "It was a dull hearing," the *Sudbury Citizen* reported. "No outbursts from the audience."

There would be plenty of outbursts later on. On September 30, nationally-known nutritionist Dr. Jean Mayer was the guest preacher at the First Parish Church. He delivered a hellfire and brimstone sermon deploring the attitude of Boston Edison and other corporate giants.

"In this case, what do we have?" He roared. "A large monopoly which could not care less what the citizenry of this town wants, which blatantly circumvents the law by taking the proposed line out of its natural way to include a little bit of Wayland, Concord and Acton so as to place this town in a minority position, and which haughtily rejects the most generous propositions made by this town...

"The famous dictum of the 19th Century railroad baron 'the public be damned' is echoed by the Boston Edison though in a more hypocritical form."

(Ironically, just a few years before, Mayer was leading the charge for the fluoridation of the town water supply over the objections of Christian Scientists and other civil rights groups).

After describing the success of Boston Edison stock during the previous year (a 2 1/2-1 split the previous June), Mayer continued:

"It is thus, I think, a fair statement to say that if the Boston Edison Company is ready to antagonize a whole community, desecrate a national wildlife refuge, blight the beauty of one of the few unspoiled spots in this area and blight a famous historical spot, it is not doing it because of stringent economic necessity."

Edison received a setback two weeks later when Buzzell revealed at a hearing that a little-known Massachusetts law decreed that ancient burial grounds could not be taken by eminent domain without a specific act of the Legislature. By a quirk of fate, Edison's route for the controversial line would pass directly over Rice's Indian cemetery.

The controversy faded from the headlines for nearly 18 months. There were occasional rumblings that caused the Power and

Light Committee to expand its jurisdiction to other matters in addition to the new Edison line. When things did flare up once more, the power company took a new tack, asking permission to upgrade an existing line that ran along the Boston and Maine railroad tracks and then vectored south through the marshes through Framingham to a sub-station in Medway. The DPU granted permission for the upgrade in December of 1964.

The upgrade would replace the 60-foot wooden towers with 160-foot steel towers placed at 1,000-foot intervals along a 250-foot right of way. "No way," said Sudbury. "Sue us," replied Edison. Sudbury did, and it wasn't until June 23, 1966 that the Supreme Judicial Court granted Edison permission to take land by eminent domain.

It turned out to be a hollow victory. For, while Edison could move ahead on land acquisition, the court had withheld permission for power lines to cross public ways without permission. If a majority of the towns involved refused this permission, Edison could not proceed.

Chairman of the Board of Selectmen John Taft announced that Sudbury would not grant permission under any circumstances, and was hopeful that Wayland and Concord would follow suit and provide the majority. He needn't have worried. Six towns ultimately joined in the fight and both the Mass. Division of Fisheries and Wildlife and the U.S. Department of the Interior expressed reservations about the lines crossing their land.

"Time is on our side," Taft told the *Sudbury Citizen*. "The longer we delay, the more chances that new technology will be in place to allow these lines to be buried willingly.

The controversy did spawn new subdivision regulations from the Planning Board. "Utility poles, guy wires and overhead wires for the distribution of electricity or the transfer of messages by telephone or otherwise shall not be permitted in subdivisions; all such wires shall be laid underground within the width of the street right of way. The Planning Board may permit transformers, switches and other such equipment to be placed on the ground in approved locations."

Sudbury rolled out the big guns in August of 1966, when Senator Ted Kennedy sided with the town and arranged for a letter from Secretary of the Interior Stewart Udall opposing the lines. Udall wrote Taft that his agency "would not grant easements for the running of overhead lines over portions of the Great Meadows National Wildlife Refuge if doing so would significantly impair natural values including scenery, or be inconsistent with the action of local government."

Jim Sheppard, Director of the Mass. Division of Fisheries and Wildlife, which controls the Pantry Brook Wildlife Management Area, also promised full cooperation with the town

When it finally came to a vote before the Selectmen five months later, it was a foregone conclusion. No power line would cross a public way in Sudbury. Period.

Edison was back in August of 1967 with a petition to cross public ways for the new, 115,000 volt line from South Sudbury to the Concord-Maynard line. Four hundred people gave up watching the Red Sox on television to jam the hearing and make their opposition known in no uncertain terms. The *Fence Viewer* reported that, aside from statements from Edison officials, not a word was said in favor of the proposed high-tension lines through Sudbury. Edison attorney Donald R. Grant maintained that the only question at stake was whether the proposed line would be safe and whether it would "incommode" the public use of a public way.

Craig Wylie, who lived in the old Ralph Adams Cramm estate on Concord Road, referred to Edison's radio commercial which said that the cost of electricity has gone down and down and down and countered: "Let's forego the fourth price reduction and the commercial in order to pay to have the lines put underground."

"The beauty of the land is important," added Dr. Howard Emmons. "We're willing to pay the difference."

"The affair isn't over," said the *Fence Viewer* in an editorial. "But some came away from the meeting feeling hopeful that the towns may win in the end."

"The Sudbury League of Women Voters has strongly supported the placing of these power lines underground because we feel that the proposed 250-foot-wide swath, seven and one half miles long, will cause irreparable damage to the Sudbury River Valley, " said League President Carol Keefe.

"Our members fear the industrializing effect of the proposed power line route on the refuge wetlands, the adjoining uplands and the accompanying dangers of water and air pollution."

But Edison wasn't quitting. In September, 1967, it requested an exemption from zoning by-laws in Sudbury, Wayland and Concord in connection with the proposed 115,000-volt line across the towns. Sudbury opposed the petition with special Counsel Philip Buzzell presenting several witnesses. The Sudbury Power and Light Committee and Selectmen from Concord and Wayland placed statements on the record in opposition.

In November, Edison petitioned the Massachusetts Supreme Court for a Writ of Certiorari to set aside the vote of the selectmen. No action was expected until spring and when it came, Edison found itself right back where it started. Edison could take land by eminent domain, but couldn't run power lines across public ways without permission.

On January 16, 1969, the State Supreme Court upheld the DPU in its decision to exempt Edison from local zoning by-laws. But the justices refused to grant the right to cross public ways without permission in the process of building the 17.5 mile right of way from Medway through Holliston, Sherborn, Natick, Framingham and Wayland to Sudbury.

Edison started construction on the upgrade in the Stock Farm Road area but was stopped by Building Inspector Francis White. Then the company went to court and obtained permission to continue as long as no public way was crossed

Finding no further recourse in the courts, Edison turned to the

Legislature, sponsoring several bills to give the DPU the power to grant road crossings. The Sudbury Power and Light Committee vigorously opposed the bills, noting that power in the wrong hands would mean an ugly forest of transmission lines in the pristine Sudbury River Valley.

The controversy finally came to an end on September 4, 1969. Governor Francis Sargent signed a bill allowing towns to require that utility wires be buried underground. On October 1, 1970, Boston Edison announced that it would install two 115,000-volt transmission lines underground along 6.7 miles of public ways between Sudbury and Maynard and repave Mossman Road in the bargain.

The wounds on both sides healed quickly. Old timers realized that over the years, Edison has gone out of its way to support the town. When emergency classrooms were needed in 1952, during the baby boom, the company made available an unused building on the Boston Post Road. Later it sold a parcel of near-by land at a very reasonable price so that the Buddy Dog Humane Society could build a state-of-the-art headquarters building and kennel.

Was the fight worth it? Anyone who drives or walks along Sudbury streets today would have to answer in the affirmative. But much more than beauty was at stake here. What was important was the reaffirmation of the principle that brought white settlers to this valley more than three hundred years ago in the first place, the right of self-determination.

The Hosmer House

Ever since it was built sometime in the 1780s, the Hosmer House has been a part of the village life in Sudbury Center. It was there in 1797 when the First Parish Church outgrew its original meeting house and built the building that remains in use today.

The house was 100 years old when the Reverend Edwin Hosmer bought it for a dollar from the widow of James Willis and moved in with his wife and four children. One of them was Florence Armes Hosmer who lived in the house until her death in 1978 at the age of 97.

Over the years the house served as a general store, post office, cobbler shop, tavern and candy store. Evidence of all these uses can still be seen as one walks through the house, which now belongs to the town and has been lovingly restored by the Sudbury Historical Commission.

Old residents remember it as a center of creativity. Mrs. Hosmer was an artist of some renown and her older brother Albert was a talented musician with a rich baritone voice. John Powers remembers trudging home past the old brick-ender on snowy evenings and listening to Mr. Hosmer at the keyboard of his piano "filling the square with melody."

Many of the hundreds of paintings turned out by Mrs. Hosmer over the years still hang on the walls of the house and provide a window into the past. It's an honest old house, just as Sudbury is an honest old town. The two, it seems, have grown up together.
(Illustration by Richard E. Hand)

154

The '60s

Conflicts Within and Without

Sudbury shared the loss of President John F. Kennedy in the Sixties, but the decade also produced two significant conflicts, one of which pitted taxpayer against taxpayer over the question of who should have the final word in the funding of the town's schools. In the other, as noted in a previous chapter, the town emerged victorious in a long-standing battle with the Boston Edison Company over the installation of high-tension transmission lines through the Sudbury River Valley.

On other fronts, the discovery of a week-old puppy in the Town Dump triggered the founding of the Buddy Dog Humane Society; the Goodnow Library celebrated its centennial; the town built a new police station on the site of the American Legion Hall; Star Market constructed the first of what would be many shopping centers on the Boston Post Road, and Town Meeting blitzed 13 zoning regulations designed to bring some order to them; a controversy over the removal of gravel from land on Lincoln Road wound up in Superior Court and Lincoln-Sudbury Regional High School produced its first graduating class.

Sperry Rand broke ground for a research and development facility on Briardale Farm off Route 117, prompting the assessors to comment that real estate taxes had reached a limit and the town must attract additional wealth in order to continue and increase services demanded by the townspeople. These "services" included three more elementary schools (Loring, Nixon and Haynes), a new Junior High School (Ephraim Curtis), an addition to Lincoln-Sudbury Regional High School and new firehouses in North and South Sudbury.

The school population situation wasn't helped when attorneys for builder Albert Halper obtained a writ of Mandamus, over-turning a ruling by the Selectmen and allowing Halper to build on several 30,000-foot lots in Wayside Acres. Another developer, Walter Beckett, caused some controversy when he tore down Stearns' Mill on Dutton road. The mill was the oldest in the United States in continuous operation.

With the Cold War on in full force, fallout shelters were the rage. Community shelters were proposed for the Lincoln-Sudbury Regional basement and for the root cellar at the Wayside Inn. One town resident built a $200 shelter in his basement and stored his beer in it.

By 1963, the tax rate had risen to $92.50, and residents were feeling the pinch. The Finance Committee noted that: "Sudbury is now in the unique financial position of having extremely high costs and an extremely low ability to pay these costs."

Individual property values were dropping while the rising cost of owning property in town was shrinking the market of persons seeking to buy homes. "Tighten your belts," advised the Fincom. Town departments complied, but the school population kept rising and the tax rate along with it. The Fincom noted that if all money articles in the 1963 Town Warrant were passed, the tax rate would rise to $110 per thousand. The budget cutters at Town Meeting went to work and kept the rise to just $1.50

G. Paul Draheim was hired as Executive Secretary to the Selectmen at a controversial starting salary of $8,000, a hefty increase over the $5,200 he was previously paid as a replacement for Clifton Giles. Draheim was also to serve as Town Accountant. He was replaced a year later by Floyd Stiles.

The Sudbury Methodist Church moved into a new building on Old Sudbury Road that the parishioners built themselves. Walter MacKinnon moved his Red and White Grocery store from the old Post Office block beside Alexander's Automotive on the Boston Post Road to a brand-new building at the corner of Concord Road and the Post Road. He named the new store Sudbury Super Market and eventually obtained a liquor license over the objections of neighbors who claimed the store was less than 500 feet from the Congregational Church.

Herb Atkinson and his wife, owners of Sudbury Laboratories and founders of the Sudbury Foundation, donated a 12-acre strip of land adjacent to Hop Brook to the Hop Brook Conservation Area. Earlier the Atkinsons' plans to donate a 100-acre tract at the corner of Hudson and Dutton roads for a hospital and shopping center were shot down at a Special Town Meeting which refused to pass the necessary zoning articles.

Professor Sumner Chilton Powell turned his graduate student thesis at Harvard into a Pulitzer Prize winning book, Puritan Village. Powell transcribed all of the early town records and explained how Sudbury's founders adapted the Open Field system of government that they knew in England to the New World. Ten-year-old Bobby Moir was appointed "Caretaker of the Common" by the Selectmen. He later received a citation for volunteerism from First Lady, Lady Bird Johnson.

Developer Bob Quirk won a battle with the town over whether or not portions of Willis Road had earlier been abandoned. At stake were $50,000 in costs for storm drains, fire alarm system, pavement and other improvements. It was bad news for the taxpayers, who were already facing a raise in the tax rate of nearly $15.

Esther Adams retired after 42 years of teaching in Sudbury schools. And the Selectmen summed up the situation in town in two succinct paragraphs:

"In many respects, 1966 in Sudbury was similar to other recent years. The population increased about five percent, several new subdivision plans were approved by the Planning Board, about 100 new houses were built, the Annual Town Meeting required half a dozen sessions, and taxes increased.

"However, for all her 328 years and her many problems as a continually growing community, Sudbury and her citizens continue to prosper. Social and community efforts proliferated and Sudbury citizens, old and new, continued to display the friendliness that has made Sudbury such an attractive town."

Sudbury honored a hometown hero in 1966 in the person of

U.S. Marine Private Alvin LaPointe, who single-handedly captured a Viet Cong 20-millimeter cannon, rescuing his company.

The 1966 Town Meeting unanimously voted a resolution stating:

> Be it hereby resolved the citizens of the Town of Sudbury, in Town Meeting assembled, commend one 19-year-old Alvin S. LaPointe of Sudbury for an extreme act of heroism while fighting for his country and the free world on the Vietnamese battlefield.

> "Marine Private First Class LaPointe, in a show of extreme courage while his entire company was pinned down, attacked an enemy bunker during a pitched three-hour fight with North Vietnamese Army Regulars in the hamlet of Vinh Loc outside Quang Ngai City, 330 miles northeast of Saigon. LaPointe crawled to within five feet of the bunker while a buddy continued cover fire. LaPointe, to the amazement of other Marines, dived into the emplacement, landing on top of the cannon.

> Following a life-or-death, hand-to-hand struggle with the enemy, LaPointe wiped out the battery. The action by Private First Class LaPointe clearly exemplifies Sudbury's past heroes and brings new glory to a town steeped in history. LaPointe's action allowed a whole company of men to advance.

Besides the honors offered by Sudbury, LaPointe, an L-S graduate, was decorated with the Cross of Gallantry with Palms, the highest honor the Vietnamese Government can bestow. He was also nominated for the Navy Cross.

Sudbury author Grace Nies Fletcher, who wrote her seventh book, *What's Right With Today's Youth*, after two cross-country tours of the nation's schools, spoke out on education in Sudbury:

> Townspeople should more carefully scrutinize the school system instead of aimlessly stating it's the best and starry-eyed and bushy-tailed running to town meeting to OK a higher budget for bigger, better, fancier school buildings.

> Those in the know maintain there is no accurate way to meas-
> ure the quality of the school system but the sure thing is not
> to place dollars in school buildings but rather on decent
> salaries for teachers.

Fletcher was refused admission into only one school nation-
wide, and that right here in Sudbury, where the School
Committee objected to her asking the students "Do you believe
in a personal God?" The students' views on pre-marital sex
went unchallenged.

In 1967, Sudbury voters petitioned for equal representation by
population on the Lincoln-Sudbury Regional School Committee
(they got it) and Moderator John Powers lobbied for more
action and less talk at Town Meeting: "Old words are best, and
the shortest old words are the best of all." (Winston Churchill).
"The town is interested in the kernel of the argument, not the
whole cornfield.

"This year the town indicated its concern for simplicity...by
placing a by-law limitation of 15 minutes for every single
speech or presentation. Overpresentation is the graveyard of
many good prospects."

Powers' words were not heeded. It took six sessions plus a special town meeting in May to conduct the town's business. One
piece of business that did get completed was a report on revaluation of all properties in Sudbury to full and fair market
value; $12,000 was appropriated to do so.

The report noted that in other towns Sudbury's size, one third
of the tax bills remained the same, one third went up and one
third went down. Exemptions were proposed for veterans and
retirees.

Two eras ended in 1968. Lawrence Tighe was replaced as Town
Clerk by Betsy Powers and Newcomer Frank Sherman defeated John Powers in the race for moderator. Both would serve
during some of Sudbury's most tumultuous times.

Sherman's first Town Meeting as moderator was a disaster. It
took eight nights to complete the 70-article warrant because of

postponements, reconsiderations and repetition, not to mention a healthy rivalry between proponents of more and better schools and the Sudbury Taxpayers' Association, a group of budget cutters bent on keeping the tax rate as low as possible.

As an afterthought, the 1969 Town Meeting passed one other item, a resolution to question the validity of the Sentinel Anti-Ballistic Missile system.

XXII

The Old Order Changeth

Sudbury's population may have been mushrooming during the '50s and '60s, but control of the town boards remained with the old-timers. Despite the rumors of improprieties and "sweetheart" deals that surfaced from time to time (but were never proved), the old guard was rarely challenged. Most town officials and committee members were long-time residents. "We'll see to things," newcomers were told.

But that all ended in the winter of 1959 in a wrangle over a gravel pit on Lincoln road. The pit belonged to William Hellman of Lincoln Lane, who arranged with contractor Walter Beckett and John Bain of Brookline, to remove gravel for Beckett's building activities. Once the gravel had been removed, the area would be subdivided into house lots.

Earth removal came under the jurisdiction of the Zoning Board of Appeals, which denied Hellman a permit to continue removing gravel.[1] Hellman and Bain took their case to selectmen Harvey Fairbank, Lawrence Tighe and Frank Trussell, who ruled that the pit had already been in operation, although sporadically and thus was a nonconforming use. They granted their blessing for gravel removal to continue.[2]

Work went apace for several months, but another party was soon to be heard from. Neighbors along Lincoln Road and Lincoln Lane, led by Priscilla Redfield Roe and Willis Fay, objected to the noise and heavy truck traffic and started to take steps to shut the operation down.

A roadblock of baby carriages made short work of the truck problem, but a more permanent solution was needed, so all those along the road who could afford it, chipped in $100 apiece to mount a legal challenge to the Board's ruling. They also successfully sponsored an amendment to the zoning by-laws at a Special Town Meeting in late May that would put earth removal under the jurisdiction of the Board of Appeals. [3]

At this point, cooler heads prevailed and determined that the only fair way to deal with earth removal was to establish a separate board with representatives from the Selectmen, Planning Board, Board of Appeals, and two private citizens appointed by the Moderator. This Board would have the clout to close loopholes such as non-conforming use.

Late in November, the Earth Removal Committee proposed stronger earth removal by-laws for Sudbury that would set up such a board, [4] but not before an internal struggle took place amongst the Selectmen which saw Tighe clash with Trussell and Fairbank on the removal of "certain language." Just what that "certain language" was, the report does not say. [5]

At a Special Town Meeting on December 15, 1959, an earth removal law was added to the by-laws. It received immediate accolades from the Selectmen. "Over the past few years, we have proposed this amendment to take the removal of sand, gravel and loam from the Zoning Laws so the problem of non-conforming use could be eliminated," Tighe wrote. "The Lincoln Road Gravel Removal Case brought this serious problem before the town. On April 1, 1960, all earth removal operations must come before a new board appointed under this by-law, therefore, non-conforming use is no longer a question." [6]

The Lincoln Road residents' case was heard by the Middlesex Superior Court on February 18, 1960. The justice dismissed the suit, but noted that Hellman, Beckett and Bain were probably in violation of one or more of the Town's zoning by-laws. The Court did grant a writ of Mandamus to the plaintiffs which essentially told the Selectmen to do their job and shut the operation down if the proper town board determined that a violation did indeed exist.

Beckett and Bain went back to the Board of Appeals, which refused to authorize further digging, and made sporadic requests to the new Earth Removal Board over the next two years to remove 100,000 yards of gravel. All their requests were denied.

In the end, much more was at stake in the gravel case than the disposition of 100,000 cubic yards of gravel or a few house lots.

"It was the end to Good Old Boy government," said John Taft. "All three Selectmen involved in the 1959 decision were out of office within three years.

"The Hellman gravel suit ties in with the coming to power of the new people. They were tired of the cronyism that had prevailed. The case taught the newcomers who were fighting the establishment of old-timers that they could fight and win."

And so it was. Tighe managed to squeak out a narrow victory over Ed Kreitsek in 1960, but Ed Moynihan defeated Trussell in 1961, Kreitsek topped Parker Albee after Fairbank announced his retirement in 1962, and Dick Venne beat Tighe handily in 1963. The old order had given way to the new.

XXIII

"We'll Sue The Town!"

The preface of the 1963 Finance Committee report was the ultimate in understatement. "Sudbury has begun to feel the impact of its rapid growth...," it said in part.

A year later, the Fincom was ready to do something about that "impact." It had developed a plan to spread the cost of schools and other Town services over a seven-to-ten-year period in order to limit tax increases to an affordable $10 a year.

In terms of "pocketbook reality," the committee reported, a $10 increase would mean an additional year-end tax payment of approximately $75 and a continuing $6.25 monthly increase for the average taxpayer. The average residential assessment in 1964 was approximately $7,500, with roughly 70 percent of all residential properties in town falling within the $5,000 to $9,000 range. Sudbury was already spending $585 a year per elementary school pupil and $850 per high school student. The national average was $435 and $566.

The rumblings about possible school budget cutbacks on the Town Meeting floor had been going on all winter and two Fincom members, Daniel P. Jameson and George F. Miller, had resigned. As the March 4th Annual Town Meeting drew nearer and nearer, it became clear that what was at stake was $16,700 and a matter of principle.

The basic facts in the case were these: since a large area of Sudbury was owned by the federal government, Sudbury received federal school aid to make up for property tax dollars lost. The School Committee had been using some of this money as a contingency fund. When the FinCom discovered this fact, it cut the school budget by $16,700, claiming that all federal funds had to be spent in the year that they were granted.

There was more at stake for the School Committee than just

the money. Under Chapter 71, Section 34 of the General Laws of Massachusetts, the Town was obligated to supply "an amount of money sufficient for the support of the public schools as required by this Chapter." In other words, what the School Committee wanted, the School Committee got. The law even provided a 25 percent penalty in the event that the Committee had to take the Town to court.

In this case, what the School Committee wanted was $16,700. If they didn't get it, they said, two elementary school teachers and two specialists would not be hired.

The atmosphere at Town Meeting was tense. After much discussion, the budget was passed with the cut intact. The following session, a motion for reconsideration of the budget was lost, 412-190. School Committee Chairman Lawrence "Bert" Tighe immediately announced that the School Committee had voted unanimously to take the Town to court.

The announcement created an uproar. It was clear that the majority of the voters wanted fiscal control and the final word. "The educational process is not a blank check," said Fincom Chairman George MacKenzie. "The School Committee will endanger the whole school system we have already spent so much to protect."

But the supporters of the school system and education in Sudbury were adamant. Nineteen taxpayers signed on as plaintiffs and the Massachusetts Teachers Association hired attorney William O'Keefe to prosecute the suit.

O'Keefe met with 75 taxpayers and declared the suit an open-and-shut case. He explained that the School Committee budget is untouchable by any local forces such as the Finance Committee. He elaborated that courts interfere with School Committee decisions only when the committee assumes power it has never been granted, or in cases of dishonesty. "The courts have ruled that the place to correct mistakes is the ballot box, not the courts," he said. Shortly thereafter, the School Committee announced it would hire teachers as if the $16,700 shortfall had been voted.

Attorney Henry W. Hardy signed on to defend the Town, but held out little hope. Unless the Town could come up with something "different and substantial," he said, he would just be going through the motions.

As Spring turned into summer, the issue divided the town. Selectman Chairman Ed Kreitsek announced he would absent himself completely from all aspects of the Town's defense. "I have stated publicly that I think that Town Meeting acted improperly and I am intellectually and in conscience convinced that for the preservation of orderly government the taxpayers' petition should be favorably acted upon by the court," he said.

On the other side of the fence, Moderator John Powers thundered: "It is the principal responsibility of elected officials to heed the will of the majority." His remarks drew fire from opponents and neutrals alike.

One of the first casualties was Superintendent of Schools C. Newton Heath, who resigned effective the end of the school year. "It is with deep regret that I am forced to accept the fact that the contradictory pressures brought to bear upon the administration by citizen minority groups and segmented school committee actions makes it impossible for me to maintain a stable and sound school system and to meet the problems of budget preparation, staff needs, curriculum development, districting and staff morale," said Heath. He was replaced by Calvin E. Eels, formerly the Director of Curriculum for the Portland, Maine, schools, but retained his post as Superintendent of Lincoln-Sudbury Regional High School.

Perhaps a letter to the editor of the *Sudbury Citizen* put it best. Entitled "Hard Times," it noted that $19,000 had been lopped from the Park and Recreation budget, and pointed out that the Town had no swimming facility or tennis court despite the fact that, for a third of the year, the kids weren't in school.

"In the action on the school budget, the Town was saying in essence--hard times are upon us," the letter went on. "We must economize and make do with less than the best, for we just cannot afford the best.

"If the School Committee and those who want good schools do not heed this fair warning, if they cannot grasp this simple statement of fact, then the people of Sudbury will have no choice but to elect the 'economy firsters' to the School Committee, then see what happens to our schools!"

Early that June the Town answered the petition of the group of 19 in the school suit and pulled a rabbit out of a hat. The Town's position, as filed by Special Counsel Hardy, would be based on two points: first, consistently rising per-pupil costs in the Sudbury school system were not justified by rising costs or the town's requirements for schools, and, unless checked, would place an intolerable burden on the taxpayers; and, secondly: "The School Committee is obligated to use federal aid for the relief of the tax burden, not as a contingency fund," he announced. "The School Committee has more than $20,000 in Federal funds that could be applied toward the alleged $16,700 deficit."

Hardy explained that Public Law 874 provides federal aid money for local schools because of tax revenue lost when federal property is located within the town. This money, given as a relief to the tax burden, is not a contingency fund to be used at the School Committee's discretion. Even though $48,000 was applied to the budget, an additional $20,142.42 remained in the fund. More than enough, he emphasized, to cover the deficit.

The local educational authority, in this case the School Committee, is responsible for counting the children and applying for the federal aid. Children of federal employees must amount to at least three percent of the school's population in order for the town to qualify for federal aid.

The petition of the 19 taxpayers, filed by O'Keefe, based its claim on precedent established under Massachusetts law that the town must appropriate whatever funds the school committee deems necessary. The taxpayers' petition, which was filed in equity court in April, contained 11 points, eight of which established the "facts" in the case. The other three asked the court to act and restore the school budget to the figure originally requested by the School Committee.

The school suit was heard by Cambridge Superior Court in late November. After initially reserving his decision, Judge Frank W. Tomasello, in a somewhat convoluted opinion, ruled that the Town must pay $16,700 plus 25 percent penalty. Backing his ruling with a four-point brief. He found that:

1--The School Committee budget submitted to the Finance Committee was reduced $16,700 by the Town Meeting, and that figure had not been restored.

2--Federal funds granted under Public Laws 86 and 87 were more than ample to satisfy the $16,700 deficiency.

3--On November 23, 1964 when the case was heard, the School Committee had expended and committed $11,160.01 of this and had an uncommitted sum of $3,934.64 on hand.

4--The School Committee had acted in good faith in its submission of its budget estimate and that the deficit of $16,700 is necessary to fulfill the Committee's obligation in the operation of Sudbury public schools.

Based on these facts, the *Fence Viewer* reported, Judge Tomasello ruled that the School Committee acted within the statutory requirements in its submission of its estimate; that the Committee was solely empowered to determine the needs of the schools; that Town Meeting acted without right in its reduction of the budget; and that there is a deficit that should be restored.

The dancing in the streets didn't last long. Early in December, the Selectmen voted unanimously to appeal the school decision to the Massachusetts Supreme Judicial Court. Selectman Ed Kreitsek, who had previously absented himself from suit decisions, joined with Dick Venne and John Taft, saying there was a fine point in the case which has never been treated by the high court. "I too, am very anxious to get an answer," he said.

Hardy announced that the appeal would be based on Judge

Tomasello's failure to rule on the intent of Public Law 874 under which towns are granted federal funds for school support. He asserted that all federal funds must be spent the year they are received and not held in a contingency fund. He estimated that the appeal would cost the town between $2,000 and $2,500.

The appeal was heard in September 1965, but the good news for the Town didn't arrive until February 23, 1966 when Justice John V. Spalding reversed Judge Tomasello's decree.

At issue, he said, was the disposition of federal dollars. In 1964 the Town Meeting refused to vote full appropriation, cutting the School Committee's request by $16,700 on the grounds that the committee was withholding federal funds to pay for unanticipated expenditures throughout the year.

Spalding, speaking for the Court, ruled that federal funds must be expended for current expenses of the school system. Money must go into the town treasury as a separate account and be expended by the School Committee without further appropriation.

The Court found that the Committee had withheld about $20,000 to purchase equipment and cover unforeseen circumstances not listed in the annual budget presented to the Town. "No authorization exists for the expenditure of federal funds in the manner in which the committee has expended them, namely for unanticipated and unlisted items," Judge Spalding decreed.

The Supreme Judicial Court further pointed out that this ruling in no way impaired or limited the traditional authority of the School Committee to decide the financial needs of its school system and establish its budget. It affected only the way in which the committee accounted for its expenditures and how federal monies were to be applied. [1]

"It was a small amount of money, but it was the principle of the thing," Powers recalled later. "Can you successfully challenge a school committee? The thinking and the case law said no. We won it and that [the federal aid money] was the crack in the armor."

The suit had a profound impact on the relationship between the Finance and School Committees. While noting that Sudbury Schools already exceeded nearly all standards of the Willis Report, a document referred to by one state legislator as "the fur coat, pearl necklace and mink stole for the school system," Mackenzie offered an olive branch:

"In part, the Finance Committee has contributed to this problem (the School Committee continuing to ask for more money, per pupil, and absolute dollar costs going up in the face of predictions of declining school enrollment) by continually maneuvering for cost reductions in other town services to compensate for tax rate increases generated by the school systems.

"We have, however, arrived at a point where no further economies are advisable if we consider the longer term development of the community. Also, this is not to imply that the schools have been uncooperative.

"This is not a recommendation to scuttle the system or to retreat from high standards. It is suggested that greater efficiencies be introduced, that budgets be based only on absolute need and not include options for duplications and that non-educational costs or factors with only marginal educational implications be reduced or eliminated entirely in certain cases.... School Committee members must be elected who are willing and capable of exercising financial responsibility as well as educational responsibility." [2]

MacKenzie's words fell on deaf ears. In the winter of 1969, faced with a $25 per thousand tax increase, the citizens of Sudbury took matters into their own hands. SAVE Fiscal Sanity in Sudbury, the first of several taxpayers' organizations, was formed and budget hearings and town meetings would never be quite the same again."

XXIV

Four Days When Time Stood Still

It was one of those steel-gray days in late November that spoke of colder weather and a long, hard winter to come. Most of the leaves were already off the big maple tree in Rodney Hadley's back yard. He was whiling away the early afternoon by raking them up and dumping them by the wheelbarrow-full on the compost heap behind his carriage house.

Rodney was the second generation of Hadleys to live at 308 Concord Road. His father, Frank Hadley, spent most of his 94 years there. Before he died in 1950, he could be found sitting beside the pitcher pump on the front lawn and offering tumblers of ice-cold well water to passersby.

Rodney, like has father before him, was sexton of the First Parish Church, responsible for janitorial duties and seeing that the clock in the steeple--which belonged to the Town--was set and operating properly. For this extra service he was paid $25 a year. The large brass key to the church, on its wrought iron ring, hung on a nail inside Hadley's back door.

Hadley was just putting the wheelbarrow away when the news came. He glanced at his watch as he listened to the emergency bulletin which interrupted the regular programming on his kitchen radio. At exactly 2 p.m. on the 22nd of November, 1963, President John Fitzgerald Kennedy had died, assassinated on the streets of Dallas, Texas.

The word spread all over town in different ways. Former High School Principal Alan Flynn heard it on the television at his Goodman Hill home and started across the street to get his mail. When the mailman asked why there were tears in his eyes, he simply said: "The President has been assassinated."

Ed Kreitsek heard the news at work in the Raytheon building and immediately called fellow Selectmen Ed Moynihan and

Dick Venne. "I just couldn't accept the fact of what I was hearing," he said later. "It was a period of no authority. You wondered how you'd get started again."

While the Selectmen were conferring and drafting a proclamation for a day of mourning, Hadley was taking matters into his
own hands. Removing the church key from its peg, he slowly
walked across the common, let himself in, climbed the stairs to
the clock tower and turned off the switch. For only the second
time in more than a century, the hands stood frozen in time.
Ninety-eight years before, they had been stopped for the death
of another champion of freedom, President Abraham Lincoln.

The streets of the town were deserted as people remained glued
to their television sets and radios for more news as the
President's body was returned to Washington on Air Force One
and taken to the White House. But, behind the scenes, plans
were being made. "In recognition of the sorrow of the people of
the nation and of the Town of Sudbury," the Board of
Selectmen, at a special meeting at 9 p.m. Saturday, November
23rd, 1963, issued the following:

Proclamation

Monday, November 25th, 1963 is hereby proclaimed a holiday
of mourning in the Town of Sudbury as evidence of the sorrow, shock and grief that overwhelms the nation upon the
death by assassination of the 35th President of the United
States, John Fitzgerald Kennedy. The somber sadness occa-
sioned by the tragic loss of our president will be evidenced by
the cessation of all municipal, civic, industrial and commercial activities on this day.

The reservation of this day to a period of mourning for John
Fitzgerald Kennedy symbolizes our dedication to the precious
principals of our constitutional government and is a demon-
stration of our heartfelt awareness of the untimely loss of a
great president whose experience and patriotic leadership
have been denied to the United States and the free world.

John Fitzgerald Kennedy's personal sacrifice to the nation is
equalled only to the immeasurable loss to his family of a loving husband and father.

For the people of Sudbury, we extend our woefully inadequate condolences to the family of the ex-president John Fitzgerald Kennedy.

We pledge our support to President Lyndon B. Johnson who, with the help of God and the people of this nation, will assume for all Americans the tremendous obligations, responsibilities and authority as the 36th President of the United States.

Proclaimed this 23rd day of November, 1963 in Sudbury, Massachusetts.
Edward F. Moynihan, Chairman
Edward E. Kreitsek
Richard C Venne

It would take more than words to reassure the townspeople that, just as it had in wars in which Sudbury soldiers were involved, life would go on as it had before. When word came of an interfaith service for the President at 5 p.m. Sunday afternoon, November 24, both floors of the Town Hall were filled within minutes and the overflow had to listen to the singing and psalm reading from the hallway and the stairs. Uniformed Boy Scouts sat in a body. Fire and police officers attended in full dress uniform.

The only speakers were the members of the clergy: Methodist minister Blaine Taylor, Father Robert Hurley of Our Lady of Fatima, Rev. Carl Scovel of the First Parish Church Unitarian, Rev. E. William Simmerman of United Presbyterian, Rabbi Zion of Congregation Beth El, Rev. Ernest Bodenweber of Memorial Congregational and Rev. Edwin Sunderland of St. Elizabeth's Episcopal.

Ministers read psalms, a hymn was sung and a bidding prayer was led by Rev. Sunderland in which the congregation stood and prayed in silence. The Proclamation from the Selectmen was read and the congregation filed slowly out into the night. The service had lasted exactly one half hour.
As the townspeople streamed to their cars, the church bell tolled in an ancient custom peculiar to Sudbury: three times three, indicating a man had died, and then 46 strokes, one for each year of his life.

It was not as much the ceremony itself as the way that the townspeople silently gathered together to reassure one another and move   on that was striking. Donald B. Willard, Publisher of the *Fence Viewer*, said it best in an editorial:

> ...The leaders of the government reacted with speed, dignity and authority. Power passed from one hand to another instantly as a matter of course, without dissent. This was only what we expected in such a case, but nevertheless it was a great good.
>
> Such a transition is possible in only a few countries in the world. It occurs here because we have acquired political skill. Much of the learning was done centuries ago in these very towns of Massachusetts. A Congress is only an elaborate kind of Town Meeting and Town Meetings too can act with celerity when need arises.
>
> ...No earthquake can shake town government and, we see again, none can shake the national government. Both are fixed by accepted rule and by common consent. And common consent is a firmer base for power than ever a dictator or emperor possessed.
>
> Even though the house be solid on its foundation, the cynic says there may be shady business in the back room. So there may. But over last weekend we saw all leaders with sober faces going about their duties, their better natures showing.
>
> "For renewed proof that our institutions are strong and that men are capable of rising to an occasion with good will, we may draw confidence and courage. [1]

"For the first time in the history of the Town, all faiths of the town were gathered together in the face of an eternal assault upon truth," John Powers was to write later. "Gone was the old factional strife. Gone was the thoughtless division of faith. As the cold winter wind grew from the west, many of those who rested on the ancient burial hill must have wondered ancient thoughts. Could the old differences be buried? Could the old codes of acceptance, or indeed, any codes of acceptance be forgotten? Was there, amidst the frightening reports of what had happened, a last chance at rededication?" [2]

Indeed there was, and from all over town the silent throng had gathered to bear witness.

On the following Tuesday afternoon, Rodney Hadley was once again raking leaves in his back yard as if nothing unusual had happened in the last four days. Looking at his pocket watch, he noticed that it was five minutes to two. Putting down his rake, he strode into the kitchen, took the church key once more from its peg, walked across the Common and re-started the town clock. The last four days would never be forgotten, but life in Sudbury, and in the nation, would go on.

XXV

A Dog Named Buddy's Legacy

Taking a shortcut through the town dump on a late Saturday afternoon was a regular routine for the boys of North Sudbury and this Saturday in late March of 1961 was no exception. Saturday was the busiest day of the week at the dump and it was always worth a quick look to see what "treasure" might have been abandoned by the more well-to-do residents from the south side of town.

The dump was actually a depleted and abandoned sand pit that the Town was slowly filling up with trash. It bore no resemblance to today's landfills. Townspeople simply backed their cars to the edge of the pit and tossed their trash down the slope. Every once in a while, someone would touch a match to the mess and the resulting fire would last for days.

The boys climbed down to the bottom of the pit and started working their way diagonally across its face. The pickings looked pretty slim. No abandoned bikes or broken lawn mowers that could be easily fixed and sold for a couple of bucks. Nothing but paper bags full of trash.

Suddenly one of the boys stopped in his tracks and cupped a hand behind his ear. "Hear that?"

"What?"

"Sounds like a baby crying. Do you hear it?"

Spreading out, the boys followed the cries to a burning brown paper bag. In it they discovered a half-frozen, two-day-old black puppy, it's hair singed by the flames. Running home, they enlisted the aid of their parents and delivered the pup to Dog Officer Harry Rice on Water Row. Rice pointed the finger of suspicion on a Sudbury resident.

"This is not the first occurrence of this kind in the area," Rice told the *Fence Viewer*. "About a year ago a mother beagle and her brood of newborn puppies were found at the Wayland town dump. The mother managed to chew her way out of the shopping bag and thus, she and her babies were saved. A few years ago in North Sudbury, puppies five to six weeks old were found abandoned by the side of the road."

The little pup, nicknamed "Buddy," quickly became the talk of the town and the Rice phone rang off the hook with requests for progress reports. Rice fed it milk every hour but had a terrible time finding a rubber nipple for a doll's bottle. The plastic nipple commonly sold with these toys didn't have enough "give" to allow the milk to come through.

"Sure, some people will say I should have disposed of the dog as soon as I received it, but the brutality behind the act got under my skin and I'm trying to save the pup." he said. "I hope public disclosure of this brutality will bother the conscience of the person who did it, maybe bother his wife a bit, because, I didn't know we had human beings as low as this around here. It's completely unnecessary in this day and in this area to have to resort to such heartless means to dispose of an unwanted creature."

Buddy's plight made the front page of the *Fence Viewer* on April 6 along with the announcement of a $50 reward offered by an anonymous Sudbury resident for the identity of the person who left the pup at the dump. Rice announced that it was a close squeak, but he thought the pup would live.

Rice explained that regulations provided that he keep stray or unclaimed dogs from five to seven days before sending them to the Harvard Medical School for experimentation. He admitted that he often kept them longer--and even bought a few-- because many are potentially excellent pets.

When a private person turned in a dog to the dog officer, the owner paid $1 a day until the dog was placed. Since neither the town or county had funds to pay the expenses of humane extermination, many dogs wound up at Harvard, something Rice said he didn't like to see.

Buddy died suddenly, barely two weeks after being found, but his passing heightened the sensitivity to the fate of stray dogs in Sudbury. On April 20, a letter to the editor of the *Fence Viewer* suggested the formation of a humane league to pay for euthanasia and cremation. By the Fourth of July, the Buddy Dog Humane Society had been founded with Alfred Halper as President, John Powers as Clerk and Augustus F. Doty, Mrs. Henry L. Nelson, Mrs. Ernest Lukas and Ed Kreitsek as charter members.

"Our basic goal is to give a new lease on life by staying execution to dogs who are friendly or healthy, and, for one cause or another, in the pound," Halper explained. "Among our long-range plans is the formation of a Buddy Dog chapter in every Massachusetts city and town--and eventually all over the United States--which will care for the dogs in its local pound."

Halper noted that, under current law, these animals are sent to vivisection hospitals or put to sleep. Buddy Dog began purchasing dogs just before their seven-day grace period was up. In less than a month with no fanfare or publicity it had already found homes for ten of the 12 "Buddy Dogs" thus far purchased.

The entry of Buddy Dog's "Stop The Executions" float in Sudbury's Independence Day parade marked the official opening of a concentrated drive for additional membership and funds to extend the pilot Sudbury program to other areas in the Commonwealth. Halper kicked off the fund drive with a $1,000 donation.

Plans called for a public relations program to elevate "Buddy Dogs" to the social strata enjoyed by their pedigreed brothers and sisters. Local branches would be established across the state and a central clearinghouse would transfer dogs from "surplus" areas to "demand" areas. Rice was delighted: "It's like a dream that has finally come true," he said.

The dream didn't waste much time becoming reality. Buddy Dog established a temporary shelter for homeless dogs on Rice's farm on Water Row. By December, the Society had placed nearly 60 dogs in good homes. Eighty percent were rescued from local pounds just before their day of execution and the additional 20 percent were left by distressed owners.

Word of the Association began to spread across New England. After Rice and Lillie Nelson appeared with a basket of puppies on the WHDH-TV Key Club Show, eight ladies from Winchester arrived one morning with dog food and cash for care and comfort of recently rescued dogs.

In 1964 the Society's headquarters moved to the Betsy DeWallace property on Dakin Road in North Sudbury while the search for a permanent home continued. The 1971 Town Meeting granted a zoning by-law change that would allow the Society to build its headquarters in a business zone, but it wasn't until December 17, 1975 that ground was broken for the present state-of-the-art kennel facility on Route 20 near the Wayland line. The land was purchased at a very favorable price from Boston Edison, and a great deal of the physical labor was supplied by volunteers.

When the new kennel opened in 1976, current Managing Director Michael Courchaine came aboard as an intern and immediately started organizing a program for the placement of cats as well as dogs. The cat program ran unofficially for ten years before an official policy was established for cats in 1986, the Society's 25th anniversary year.

"Over these years our policy has not changed," said Kreitsek. "For homeless dogs we provide warm shelter, food, medical care, grooming and attendants who really care. There is no limit to how long our guests stay with us. We will care for them until the right adoptive owner comes to claim them. Many dogs live with us for months, some have for a year or longer, and then find a loving new home to share in return for affection, gratitude and loyalty."

The Society established a spay-neuter program in the early '80s, and, by 1998, no animal leaves the kennel until it has been spayed or neutered. Today Buddy Dog accepts more cats than dogs and finds homes for more than 2,500 animals a year. "Buddy's" legacy lives on.

The Goodnow Library

John Goodnow was a rich and ambitious man, but he had a soft spot in his heart for two things: his native town of Sudbury and the education of its children.

Goodnow, the son of John Goodnow the centenarian, lived on Landham Road in East Sudbury and established a large importing firm with the aid of his brother, George. The firm did a brisk trade in the West Indies and soon amassed a huge fortune. When he died, he left a bequest in his will to establish a public library, which would become only the second free library in the Commonwealth of Massachusetts.

The bequest left $2,500 and three acres of land for a suitable building and grounds as well as a $20,000 endowment, the income of which was to be used for operating expenses. The octagon-shaped building, designed by Joseph R. Richardson of Boston, was finished in 1864 at a total cost of $2,691.35 which included setting out the beautiful maple shade trees, some of which still stretch back to Hop Brook.

Samuel Puffer was the low bidder for the post of librarian and had the responsibility for 2,300 books. Additional volumes soon created a space problem and the main reading room was constructed in 1895 for $5,895.85, using savings from the Goodnow Trust Fund.
(Illustration by Davis)

The '70s

HORNETS UNDER SUDBURY'S COATTAILS

Just who first spotted it on an early summer evening in 1970 is somewhat of a mystery, but word of the discovery spread rapidly across the town. The Revolutionary War Memorial, which had stood since June 7, 1896, on the little knoll between Mount Pleasant Cemetery and the Town Hall, had a large gray paper nest of white-tailed hornets firmly ensconced under its Quincy granite coattails!

That hornets nest said a lot about Sudbury in the 1970s, a time when inflation, controversy, fuel shortages, high taxes and scandal not only swept the nation, but settled very close to home as well.

The 70s saw a controversial transfer of power in the police department with Sergeant Nick Lombardi taking over for veteran chief John McGovern, who had served for 26 years and expanded the police force from a single officer to 21 men. It took three years, three town meetings, a power struggle by the Selectmen and a secret ballot to solidify Civil Service status for the Chief of Police.

At a Special Town Meeting on November 1, 1971, the Selectmen petitioned to have the Chief's job taken off Civil Service so that they could go outside the department to broaden the field of candidates. They were denied by a 443-339 vote. Not to be deterred, they came back at the Annual Town Meeting the following April with a by-law establishing a police department and removing the chief from Civil Service. It passed. Two weeks later, a reconsideration vote was just ten votes short of the required two thirds.

The issue, which hinged on just who had or had not passed the Civil Service exam, was finally settled by secret ballot at a Special Town Meeting called for May 30, 1972. After considerable debate the position of Chief of Police was put back on Civil Service by a 400-297 vote.

It would be nearly two years before Lombardi was officially appointed Chief. In the meantime, Sergeant Peter Lembo filed suit against the Selectmen, claiming that he was the only member of the force to pass the Civil Service exam. The tests were re-evaluated and it was revealed that Lombardi and Sergeant Wesley Woodward had also passed.

Lombardi had no sooner taken his permanent seat at police headquarters when controversy broke out on several other fronts. With Watergate, the oil crisis, runaway inflation, and a deepening recession, putting pressure on the tax rate, a group of seven men formed the Sudbury Taxpayers Association which soon ballooned to more than 600 members and became a moving force in the reduction of town spending between 1974 and 1976. The tax rate held steady in 1974 and actually dropped $2.50 in 1975.

Sudbury was moving on another front to relieve more pressure on its taxpayers. Faced with the loss to reapportionment of hundreds of thousands of dollars of state aid for the schools, not to mention Governor Mike Dukakis's "appropriation" of $50 million of town and county funds to balance the state budget, Sudbury filed a class action to force all cities and towns in Massachusetts to base their tax rates on full and fair valuation.

The Selectmen explained that ever since Sudbury went to full and fair valuation in 1970, taxes had increased from $37 a thousand in 1970 to $49.50 in 1973. They also pointed out that Sudbury's Cherry Sheet (school) aid was down by approximately $460,000 over that period because the town was assessed at full and fair market value.

"Cities and towns who have obeyed the Commonwealth's law on full and fair valuations are already being punished by lower distributions under programs such as Chapter 70 School Aid and the Lottery, since the amount of money a city or town receives is in reverse relation to valuation," [1] wrote Executive Secretary Ed Thompson, who had replaced Floyd Stiles on October 9, 1972.

"Sudbury plans a class action suit petitioning for all towns in the state to go on full market value. It is one of 44 communities out of 300 in the Commonwealth which have complied with the law."

"Sudbury, as are all similar suburban communities, is getting the short end of the stick," echoed the Selectmen. "We get little comparative return as a result of recent state aid formulas as well as revenue sharing and new federal grant programs. The Selectmen are continuously working in every possible way to minimize the impact of the above facts." [2]

By fall of 1973, more towns joined Sudbury in the revaluation suit; Newton, Burlington and several towns outside of the South Middlesex area promised support and Town Counsel David Turner drew up a tentative outline of a Bill of Equity. Turner noted that the statute provided no remedy for the resulting inequity and penalty suffered by towns already on full and fair valuation.

The case went to the Supreme Judicial Court early in January, 1974, and Sudbury prevailed, although it would take three more years and another trip to court before many of the cities and towns that would benefit from less than full and fair valuation finally complied.

The final challenge came in October 1978, in the form of a letter from the Metropolitan Area Planning Council (MAPC) asking support for an amendment that would kill the full and fair assessment requirement. MAPC, acting in behalf of the larger cities and towns in the Commonwealth, claimed that residential taxes would rise under full and fair valuation and industrial and business taxes would fall. The proposal died on the vine.

Sudbury had a Watergate of its own in the middle of the decade when Highway Superintendent Edward Blaine was indicted on two counts of larceny, prompting a power struggle over control of the Highway Department between the Board of Selectmen and the Highway Commission. The controversy finally led to a Special Town Meeting dissolving the Commission on December 18, 1975.

The '70s were also the decade of the Bicentennial and Sudbury celebrated in grand style. Tony Moore, then Mayor of Sudbury, Suffolk, England and a guest for the festivities, called Sudbury "A good example of a well-run town." The thousands of visitors that packed the town for the three-day celebration agreed.

The decade saw the first region-wide elections for the Lincoln-Sudbury Regional School Committee, which produced the youngest winner ever in 19-year-old Bill Haas. Many Sudbury voters did not agree with the concept and sponsored a repeal article at the next town meeting. It was unsuccessful, and the concept remains in place today.

Sudbury entered into the Minuteman Regional Vocational Technical School District in 1971, and a dog control law finally passed town meeting. The first attempt to establish multi-unit zoning failed miserably in 1972, but the King Philip Road historic district was established.

In 1974 the Sudbury Companies of Militia and Minute sent the Wayside Inn's old Abbot and Downing stagecoach for a facelift at Louden, New Hampshire. The coach made a triumphant return to Sudbury behind a four-horse hitch, arriving on October 10, bearing retired postmaster Forrest Bradshaw and commemorative letters from towns all along the route.

In 1975 the School Committee negotiated the first three-year teachers' contract in the history of the town; 58 teachers sued the town for $100,000 after being notified that their contracts would not be renewed; Town Meeting sent the school budget back to the Committee asking for another $100,000 in cuts, and a large animal--thought to be a puma--killed 65 of Philip Newfell's turkeys in North Sudbury.

"SudBus," an experiment in intra-town transit service lasted for less than a year before running out of money and riders in 1975; shrinking enrollment and rising costs became a major concern at Lincoln-Sudbury; the town finally prevailed in a drawn-out bout with New England Telephone to expand local service to include bordering communities, and a study revealed that Sudbury residents had twice the average incidence of hypertension.

A shrinking population of school age children prompted a rash of school closings, starting with Horse Pond Road School in 1976 and eventually including Fairbank, Nixon and Loring as well; Sudbury weathered the Blizzard of '78 better than most of its neighbors thanks to some efficient work by the Highway Department; Florence Armes Hosmer, 97, died in 1978, leaving her house and land to the town. Members of the Historical Commission discovered more than 400 of Mrs. Hosmer's paintings in the house. Later that same year, Harry Rice died, leaving $100,000 to create a town museum to house his local American Indian artifacts. By the time the estate was finally settled, only $25,000 reached the town's coffers.

Route 20 was called the "Second Golden Mile" by some and a flat-out eyesore by others, but new limited business zoning regulations paved the way for Sudbury Crossing. As the decade came to an end, a home rule petition to increase the Board of Selectmen from three members to five was roundly defeated, a new personnel pay scale approved and cluster zoning established on a piecemeal basis.

Lincoln-Sudbury celebrated its 25th birthday amid financial controversy; Town Meeting peeled $66,000 from the elementary school budget only to reinstate it when threatened with a taxpayer suit, and the Sudbury Companies of Militia and Minute apologized to the Concord Selectmen for parading through town on April 19 without a permit.

Two thousand people showed up at a three-day rock concert and pig roast off Old County Road, creating a ticklish crowd control problem for Sudbury police and the Selectmen. The organizer later threatened to sue the town for police brutality.

XXVI

Sudbury's Bicentennial Through English Eyes

Author's Note: Anthony Moore, ex-Mayor and Town Councillor of Sudbury, Suffolk, England, filed this report to the Sudbury, England Town Council after attending Sudbury's Bicentennial activities in 1976. [1]

It was a great privilege for my wife Valarie and me to represent the people of Sudbury, Suffolk, in Sudbury, Massachusetts, USA, for the Bicentennial celebrations.

Sudbury, Massachusetts, is in that part of America called New England, close to Boston and the eastern seaboard. The community was named after our Sudbury, in honour of John Wilson, a preacher, one of the first settlers.

From the moment of our arrival at Logan Airport, Boston, where we were met, we knew we were amongst friends. We had left behind us the brashness of New York, and, at Sudbury, Massachusetts, found ourselves in a rural community not unlike our own.

Sudbury, Massachusetts, covers about 25 square miles and is set midst a forest. It is very green and at this time of year (early July) everywhere are great sweeps of orange day lily. There are a number of lakes and ponds and a large river.

The trees are mainly American oak and ash--distinguished from ours by the size. The oak leaves are the size of tea saucers and the ash in similar proportion. We were charmed by the wildlife--huge yellow butterflies, blue jays, hummingbirds and especially the chipmunks which seemed to be straight out of Bambi with a liking for salted peanuts! We saw heron and crane as well as river turtle sunning themselves on the rocks and even some snakes (non-poisonous, we were assured). But the famous all-red cardinal bird eluded us.

The houses and public buildings are all colonial or colonial-style--mainly white painted (sometimes red ocher painted) clapboard buildings with shingle roofs set in trees with no formal gardens or fences. It is a planning necessity for each house to have at least an acre of land, and most have more.

The community is obviously a prosperous one with most people working in Boston some 20 miles distant.

We found the community very conscious of the need to improve the quality of life. For instance, no advertising signs or billboards are allowed, and there is not the usual clutter of "street furniture" and even the road directional signs are chipped out of granite to please the eye (incidentally, one of the signs in Sudbury points to Acton, Newton and Ipswich!)

Our home for the stay was the Wayside Inn, one of America's historic show-places, preserved and restored and filled with antiques by the late Henry Ford and visited by such people as George Washington and the late President Kennedy, and, more recently by Paul Newman. It was the place that Longfellow stayed and wrote *Tales of a Wayside Inn*, including the famous Landlord's Tale of Paul Revere's Ride.

Throughout we were guests of the three Selectmen, that is the elected executive team who carry out the wishes of the community and oversee the day-to-day running of the town's affairs. "Town" is a misnomer for in fact the area is so vast the population of 16,000 are spread out lightly, more like Little Cornard than our own Sudbury.

The town government derives from the early settlers' determination to be ultra democratic, based upon laws of this country (England). There is an annual town meeting at which the whole community may be present--and very nearly are. School halls have to be taken to accommodate the crowd, sometimes 1,000 strong.

The Selectmen's proposals for the year form the agenda items and open discussion and voting take place point by point. Such meetings can go on for days, but it does mean the man in the street (or the man in the woods) is master of his own destiny and, it seems to us, makes for a more responsible community.

The town is somewhat autocratic, being responsible for such things as its schools, fire and police services, water supplies and the like, and, I believe, is a good example of how a community should be run. Many of the executive officers are elected and unpaid, save for expenses.

The programme arranged for us totally filled our time. On the business side we toured the town's administrative offices and met and talked with members of the departments and were given a very frank and full insight into the workings of a small American town--and ideas which might well apply to the advantage of our own community.

For instance, the Sudbury, Massachusetts town hall is almost fully used by local groups and organizations who are not charged for use. A town committee runs it and looks after the town hall and users clean up after themselves (or are otherwise prevented from free future use). The community takes care of the property because of the responsibility placed upon them. Our own town hall in Sudbury (England) is charged for (as well as being heavily subsidized) but is little used and is not always left by users in good order. Perhaps here is a germ of an idea for us.

The Sudbury library has a paperback book exchange section. People simply take a paperback book out and replace it with another--a simple and effective idea which ensures plenty of reading matter without cost to the authority. This library also has a picture borrowing scheme so that people could borrow paintings and prints to adorn their homes on a monthly exchange scheme.

We attended many receptions and dinners organized by different groups and during our stay must have met and spoken with several hundred people. On the final day at an open-air luncheon, I addressed collectively the Rotary Club, Chamber of Commerce, Lions Club and Business and Professional Women's Club, talking about our own community, and so we had the opportunity to promote our Sudbury and did so whenever the opportunity occurred as I did at the press conferences arranged and at various radio and television interviews. The New Englanders are greatly interested in England and Sudbury and our way of life and I fully expect that many people will now make an effort to visit our community when in England.

One of the great joys of the visit, especially for my wife, was to have the opportunity to go into so many American homes--some still filled with original colonial furniture, some modern, but mostly all beautiful and well cared for, and she was particularly taken by all the hand work in evidence.

On the 3rd July was a Great Ball in the centre of Sudbury, taking place at seven different venues--the town hall, church halls, school halls, etc. with a different type of dance going on in each--waltzing, jazz, the forties, Dixieland, rock and, of course, square dancing.

Some 3,500 people attended! At the opening of the ball we were escorted in procession from Heritage Park led by a local company of minutemen and a Scottish pipe band and, once the ball was underway, people promenaded from place to place under the trees on a beautiful night. That night I received my commission into the Sudbury Company of Minutemen and have a parchment certificate and a felt tricorn hat to prove it!

On July 4th 1976--the great day--we attended services at the Methodist Church, a large white boarded building with steeple and bell that had been constructed by the townspeople themselves in the early days. Everyone, congregation, ministers and choir, were in colonial dress and the church was overflowing.

The service, a spirited rededication to Independent America, was moving and patriotic and we shall never forget the choir's rendering, accompanied by organ, fifes and drums, of the Battle Hymn of the Republic. I think there was not a dry eye in the church.

Following the service, the town met in a newly-formed bicentennial park--Heritage Park--in the town centre by a lake and there we planted a tree commemorating our visit. The Declaration of Independence was read and at 2 p.m. precisely, the Stars and Stripes was unfurled to the ringing of bells--at that moment in time being rung in noisy celebration throughout America.

There followed a presentation ceremony under the portico of the whiteboard town hall. The chairman of the Selectmen was clearly touched by the message on Mr. Louis Prince's illuminated address from our town to theirs and referred to our common heritage.

The bronze Gainsborough horse also presented was appreciated and will find a prominent place in Sudbury, Massachusetts to stand as a permanent advertisement for Sudbury and for Gainsborough's House. We received on behalf of our town a specially leather bound and illuminated book on *The History of Sudbury, Massachusetts.*

July 5th was taken up by the crowning of the Bicentennial queen (who we had helped select earlier in the week) and then the grand parade. Some 100 floats stretched for three miles and many were enormous. It seems that people living in a particular neighborhood or street worked together to make their float as well as entries from civic organizations and sports groups. Various departments of the town administration each had an entry.

The vast parade attracted thousands of people from great distances. The parade was led by the scouts carrying a banner with the two Sudburys' coats of arms followed by the Union Jack and the Stars and Stripes side by side. This was followed in turn by the three Selectmen and myself with Valarie and the three Selectmen's wives driven in an open car behind. Then followed the parade.

Several thousand people lined the roadway which made us feel very happy. At the Town Hall we watched the parade go past and could not help but marvel at all the work it represented.

One of the items in the parade carried by children was a large woven banner showing the bicentennial flag. After the parade and speeches, this was given to me by the children who made it for the children of Sudbury, Suffolk. The children expressed the hope that they might find pen friends. I feel sure that now contact has been made, especially by the children, it must be maintained. I hope that the schools will be proud to cooperate to this end. I am sure there is much to be learned from one another and the advantage of a common language is obvious. There was some talk of school exchange visits being arranged.

These are just a few of the events. There was so much more. A river cruise from Sudbury to Concord through Indian village sites, a childrens' dog show, the Miss Bicentennial Year competition, picnics, barbecues, swimming parties, receptions at the British and Canadian consulates and, to our particular delight, Colonial Night at the Pops conducted by the aged Arthur Fiedler.

We saw the Red Sox play baseball, had lunch at the top of a skyscraper, visited the coast at Cape Cod (the Moby Dick and Kennedy family home), went to the island of Martha's Vineyard where "Jaws" was filmed (must go back and tell the children we had a dip in shark-infested waters!) and even on the way home managed the top of the Empire State Building in New York.

One memorial day was a trip to the State House in Boston and a meeting with the Governor of Massachusetts, Michael Dukakis and it was wonderful to tell him that the first Governor of Massachusetts, John Winthrop from Groton, trod the earth in our town.

All these things impressed us, but the most lasting impression is the kindness of the people and their pride in having English connections and in these days when we watch and read so much about this country's (Britain) lack of prestige, it was good to find Great Britain held in such high esteem, at least in the part of the world we visited.

We did what we could to maintain that esteem--mainly by avoiding the powerful American cocktails--and we learned what we were able to learn and experience on this visit which may have some practical application to benefit our town.

One positive result is the formation of the Sudbury (Massachusetts) branch of the Friends of St. Peter. On the final night of our stay we hosted a "thank you" dinner for our hosts.--Anthony Moore.

XXVII

Sudbury's Little Watergate: The Highway Commission Affair

The Highway Commission had never been a popular institution in Sudbury. According to the Selectmen, they were accountable to nobody but the voters; the voters didn't like them because somebody else's potholes were always being fixed before theirs, and the School Committee worried that they were spending too much of the town's money. In short, they were a loose cannon with a $750,000 budget.

The Commission had been a bone of contention in town government for many years. First proposed in 1962, it was established by a home rule petition the following year. Five years later, an article appeared on a November 28, 1968, Special Town Meeting warrant to "rescind" it. The article failed.

By 1970, the heat was on again. Highway Superintendent Louis Cassella suddenly resigned, to be replaced by Weldon Thomas, who, in turn, was replaced by Thomas McClure. Another attempt to dissolve the Commission failed in 1971.

Edward Blaine took over the following year, but his honeymoon was short. In May, 1974, Town Accountant John Wilson, in a routine audit, discovered some apparent discrepancies in highway money handling methods. After dithering for more than a month, the Commission voted to suspend Superintendent Blaine with pay, pending completion of investigations and any legal proceedings. [1]

On August 8, 1974, the Middlesex County Grand Jury indicted Blaine on two counts of larceny. In February of 1975, he was acquitted on the first; that he had allegedly kept $476 in cash receipts from rubbish collectors. Blaine's attorney, Donald Conn, charged at that trial that "someone was out to get Ed Blaine." and that charge became the basis of Blaine's later unsuccessful suit against the Selectmen for $250,000 for libel and slander.

The following June, Blaine was also acquitted of the second larceny charge--allegedly pocketing the $1,224 proceeds from the sale of scrap metal at the dump--after explaining that the scrap metal money had been used to refurbish an office at the Highway Department. [2]

The flabbergasted Board of Selectmen then released both a 1974 report by the Haskins and Sells accounting firm which cited several violations of municipal law, and a series of executive session minutes and court transcripts relating to the Blaine affair which included charges that he had used bituminous concrete earmarked for Sudbury's roads to pave the Highway Department parking lot and had not followed the proper bidding procedures for Highway Department purchases. They intimated that the Highway Commission had a thief on the payroll whom they should fire forthwith.

"Now," they said, "It's up to the Highway Commission to act."

The Commission did, the next night, by a vote of 3-1, (with Martha Coe absent and Chairman John Hare opposed) they voted to reinstate Blaine and pay him his $13,000 in back salary. [3]

Claiming that Blaine had admitted on the witness stand that he had misappropriated Town funds, the incensed Selectmen voted to secure the Blaine trial transcripts and have them sent to the Middlesex County District Attorney's office for future action. [4] None was forthcoming. The Selectmen followed up by holding a press conference and issuing a statement castigating the Highway Commission for its action. Highway Commissioner Fred Welch responded that it was all "none of the Selectmen's business" and Chairman Tony Galeota added: "It's about time we stopped taking it on the chin."

The Highway Commission did vow to run a tighter ship, and for some weeks the whole issue settled to a simmering boil, just below the surface.

But not for long. Blaine was quoted by Nick King of the *Boston Globe* as saying: "Every day I work, the Selectmen choke a little more." His lawyer called the press release: "A vendetta and political harassment designed to smoke screen the unsuccessful larceny charges and provide justification for reorganizing the Highway Department under the control of the Selectmen." [5]

At this point, Blaine was a pawn in a power struggle between the Selectmen and the Highway Commission. "Blaine was an occasion of opportunity," said a former member of the Commission. "We all knew the Selectmen were out to get the Highway Commission. A lot of it was personal and a lot the organization and structure of town government. People want things fixed, and when they do, they call the Selectmen. The Commission and the Selectmen had been at odds for a long time."

In August, Blaine brought his suit against the Selectmen. It would drag on for nearly five years before a court finally ruled that Blaine had failed to prove malicious intent by then-Chairman John Powers. Attorney David Turner defended the Town pro bono.

"That suit didn't bother us at all," Powers said later. "The Commission wasn't doing its job and Blaine was doing something that wasn't his job and they didn't have the guts to call him on it. They should have fired him right off--we told them that--but they were too lily-livered."

In September, John Hare, the only commissioner to vote against Blaine, resigned his post, pleading lack of sufficient time to serve adequately, and the preliminary hearing of Blaine's suit was called off. The attorneys, Conn said, had agreed it was unnecessary.

On October 13, 1975, the Selectmen appointed Robert Phelps to replace Hare. Phelps later told the Special Town Meeting that Highway Department employees were unhappy. Many of them were even then putting their jobs on the line by distributing leaflets outside the meeting hall.

Meanwhile the Highway Commission announced a new three-year contract with Blaine, assuring him raises over that period. The Selectmen quietly voted to call for abolition of the Highway Commission at a December 15 Special Town Meeting.

"Dissolving the Highway Commission will put out the fire of chaos and re-establish Sudbury as a well-run town," said Selectman Chairman John Taft. "It's important for the townspeople to get a chance to be heard on the way the Highway Commission has been operating over the past few months. This seems the best way to do it." [6]

Galeota jumped to the Commission's defense. "The Highway Commission is working," he said. "Just ride around town and see what we've done in the last five years. And as for Blaine's contract being for three years, the statute requires that it be for three years!" [7]

But the efforts of the Commission were to no avail. The Selectmen had whipped the voters to a fever pitch and when a request for a secret ballot was granted at the Special Town Meeting, the Commission's doom was all but sealed. As of March 26, 1976, The Sudbury Highway Commission would be history. Blaine announced he would seek another job as of March 1.

The Selectmen had the last word in the 1975 Town Report: "The townspeople's 'Vote for Sudbury' at the December 15th Special Town Meeting, will give the Highway Department, its employees and the town the opportunity for a fresh start", they wrote.

"The revelations of mismanagement and improper handling of town funds would not go away, and, once the townspeople had accepted the awful truth and witnessed the 'business as usual' attitude of the majority of the Highway Commissioners, they made their decision. The immediate reaction was one of relief, of taking a depressing weight from all of our shoulders, of putting Sudbury 'right' again."

Robert Noyes, the third generation of his family to hold the position, took over as highway surveyor on the first working day of January, 1976. He served as an elected town official until Sudbury hired Town Manager Steven LeDoux who appointed William Place to the post in 1998.

In one respect, the controversy served a useful purpose. It highlighted the advantages of consolidating day-to-day executive power with one individual rather than several boards or commissions.

XXVIII

The Good Idea That Faded Quietly Away

It started off as many things do with a phone call. Nobody remembers who called whom, but the upshot of it all was a meeting of seven Sudbury residents in Teddy Doyle's living room early in March of 1974. The seven had one thing in common. They were sick of paying high real estate taxes when few of their children were still in school to benefit from them.

Doyle was an executive at the Raytheon Corporation; Joe Buscemi, the owner of Colonial Barber Shop, was a small businessman; Don Bishop was a retired Air Force officer; Raymond Clark was an advertising executive and officer in the Sudbury Companies of Militia and Minute; Norman Peskin, Ira Potell and Leonard Sanders were ordinary citizens and taxpayers.

The Seven were concerned about the financial future of Sudbury as well as their own. The oil crisis and a deepening recession was shrinking the value of their paychecks. To complicate matters, the Commonwealth of Massachusetts had withheld $50 million in local aid to cities and towns to balance the state budget. And to add insult to injury, Town Meeting was considering a budget and several capital projects that would raise the tax rate to $65.55 if passed.

Sudbury had held the line without an increase in the tax rate, but the Selectmen were asking all town departments to level-fund their budgets and had joined with the Massachusetts Selectmen's Association to sponsor a bill that would provide some control over skyrocketing school expenses. Another group in town was drumming up support for a by-law change that would establish a five percent cap on tax increases each year.

The meeting in Teddy Doyle's living room was followed by an announcement in the *Sudbury Citizen* of the formation of the Sudbury Taxpayers' Association or STA. "We're asking for a dollar, no more, no less," said Potell, of Nobscot Road, who volunteered to be treasurer of the group. Interested townspeople

were asked to send their dollars and their names and addresses to him. Nearly 100 did within a week of the announcement.

"Their purpose is simple and single-minded," said the *Citizen*.
"To draw the line firmly on taxes. 'No more,' they say. 'Less
even.'

"And their strength, they realize, will be in numbers, and they
are asking all townspeople, regardless of political persuasion,
to join them.

"One of the members of STA put it this way: 'There's a time you
have to say "no" no matter how worthy the project or how badly
it's needed. You simply have to realize that the budget says no.
Too many people are being squeezed out of Sudbury by taxes.
Too many more are seriously considering whether the rewards
are worth the cost." [1]

Doyle explained that STA had taken no positions on any warrant article. The organization planned no formal floor presentation, but vowed to study money articles closely and to advise
and inform members and the general public of their findings.
One thing the STA would do was to encourage attendance at
Town Meeting.

"How strong STA will eventually become is, of course, anybody's guess," trumpeted the *Citizen*. "But the voice of the taxpayer is beginning to be heard throughout the land."

By the time the Association held a Sunday evening fact-finding
and strategy session at the Town Hall, membership had risen
to several hundred. The meeting decided to seek budget reductions in overall totals, instead of specific items, although there
was opposition to a walkway snowplow, septic system at Feeley
Park, intra-town bus service, walkways, drainage, Featherland
ski area, a recreation area on the Haskell Land off Fairbank
Road, a new police/fire headquarters, Town Hall renovations,
and Lincoln-Sudbury athletic field drainage.(Twenty-five years
later, the Town would have all of these and more).

"The Association is expected to commit the School Committee
budgets, both Elementary and L-S to committee and return to

the Town Meeting with a lower total," *The Citizen* reported.

"Other towns have cut school budgets and lived to tell about it," said one member. "If the School Committee accepts the town's mandate to cut the budget, there is no ground for ten taxpayers to sue their fellow taxpayers to restore the higher budget submitted originally by a School Committee."

The April 4, 1974, Annual Town Meeting opened amidst confusion as representatives of the Taxpayers Association attempted to pass wholesale cuts in the protection and highway accounts, only to be chided by Moderator Frank Sherman and Selectman John Taft.

"Nobody questions Town Meeting's right to set the budget," said Taft. "But it should behave in a responsible manner. Changes in the budget cause repercussions elsewhere and we are beginning to see that. Four years ago we found we couldn't do collective bargaining on the town meeting floor."

Finance Committee and STA member Don Bishop remarked that his quarrel wasn't with the fire department or the Fincom, but with his wallet. He suggested that town departments tighten up their budgets before the end of the fiscal year.

As the meeting wore on it became apparent that the STA would be a force to be reckoned with. The Elementary School budget was committed back to the School Committee for further cuts before squeaking by 359-337 later in the proceedings. Potell, speaking for the Taxpayers Association, revealed that the town of Groton, on two occasions, avoided taxpayers' suits by removing administrative funds from the school budget, cutting them, and voting them as a separate item. Potell added that Groton had cut administrative costs on two occasions without repercussions from the courts.

The Lincoln-Sudbury budget was approved after some strong words from Ray C. Ellis of Goodman Hill Road who termed it "the fattest in the state" with per-pupil costs of $1,714 in the '73-'74 school year.
After ten stormy sessions, it was over. Whether it was the badgering of the STA or a windfall from the State Cherry Sheet

depended upon whom you talked to, but the bottom line was the tax rate held its ground at $49.50 despite runaway inflation and recession. Now both taxpayers and town officials began to wonder just what the Association would do next.

They didn't have long to wait. At the end of the summer, the Association presented the Selectmen with a petition containing more than 600 signatures requesting that the Board NOT call a Special Town Meeting to approve funds for a Police/Fire headquarters in Sudbury Center. The Selectmen promptly rejected the petition, claiming that the signatures hadn't been certified as required by law. [2]

Undeterred, and charging harassment, the Association proceeded to certify 592 of the signatures and came marching back to the Board where a great debate ensued. "Selectmen are taxpayers too," huffed Chairman John Powers, noting that he was a former member of SAVE, a taxpayers group that had preceded the STA.

He felt the Selectmen were duty-bound to call a Special Town Meeting to allow the electorate to vote on the fire-police headquarters. He pointed out that considerable money could be saved by not waiting until the 1975 Annual Town Meeting due to rising building costs.

"The Board is in sympathy with the goal of lower taxes," he said. "And we have been busily engaged on the state and local scene striving to effect that result." He pointed out the Board's support of the class action suit requiring all towns in Massachusetts to base their tax rates on full and fair assessments, and cited efforts in progress to develop a strong capital improvement program, "which, with standardized accounting and reporting systems, and with a search for consensus on budget guidelines, should yield effective results in strengthening the management of our town business." [3]

The Taxpayers Association had the final word on October 22 when, despite the support of the Finance Committee, the joint police-fire headquarters was defeated 352-265. The Association pointed out that both departments needed new equipment more than the town needed a capital project.

In 1975, something strange began to happen. As suddenly as it appeared, the Sudbury Taxpayers Association began to fade away. Aside from one argument with the Finance Committee on an $18,000 proposal for the purchase of the Whitcomb land near the Wayside Inn grist mill for conservation purposes, the Association was heard from very little at Town Meeting. Some later attributed its demise to the fact that growth in town had temporarily peaked and personal financial problems were going away.

The tax rate dropped by $2.50 per thousand in 1976. While some gave the Association and the Fincom the credit, the real reasons were increased valuation, increased state aid and cuts in state assessments.

"For the first time in 14 years the property rate dropped," the Selectmen noted in the 1975 Town Report. "And at a substantial five percent at a time when inflation was pushing other costs of living to new heights. This $2.50 drop in the rate was no accident: once again the voters called the shots on Town spending and the successful Sudbury Equalized Valuation suit of 1974 restored over $400,000 in school aid to Sudbury."

And then came 1976, the year that Moderator Frank Sherman called "The year that nothing happened all at once." There were no controversial articles, and so few voters that Sherman proposed a by-law change that would establish the quorum at 200. "In order to be able to govern ourselves, is it necessary to have controversial articles on the warrant to attract voters?" he wondered.

Sherman didn't have the opportunity to work with a 200-voter quorum. His nine-year tenure was ended by J. Owen Todd in 1977, as were the terms of several other financial "liberals." "The election showed a definite cost-conscious mood," commented *Town Crier* columnist Arthur MacDonnell.

And perhaps that was part of the answer. Members of the Taxpayers Association moved from the outside to the inside of town government, bringing their fiscal conservatism with them; but other factors were at work as well. In the next six years, Sudbury's school population would drop from 3,059 to less than 2,000.

Perhaps the Finance Committee said it best: "The Finance Committee represents the citizens of this town in reviewing proposed expenditures," it wrote in the 1976 Town Report. "We recognize that our frustration is citizens' frustration. However, we believe that, while we lack certain statutory controls over school budget decisions, we can exert citizen pressure to be fiscally responsible.

"Specific steps are needed to make next year's cost burden smaller. Pressure on salary negotiation teams, evaluation of new or expanded programs and year-round budget reviews prior to the formulation of actual budgets are all steps leading towards achievement of fiscal responsibility."

Four years later, the voters of the Commonwealth gave that "fiscal responsibility" a boost. They overwhelmingly approved a tax-cap proposal called "Proposition 2 1/2" that limited tax increases to two and one half percent of the previous year's levy. The Sudbury Taxpayers Association was no more, but the legacy it left would remain with Sudbury and the Commonwealth for a long time to come.

The Sudbury Town Pound

You'll see it at the eastern end of the Revolutionary Cemetery in Sudbury Center, its rough stone walls forming a small square with a narrow opening toward the road just big enough for one cow or horse to pass through at a time.

It is the Sudbury town pound, one of only three such facilities remaining in Massachusetts, and technically, it is still in operation. It is the repository for stray animals found along the streets of Sudbury, and, while it doesn't get much use these days, it stands ready to confine an errant horse or cow until the police department can locate its owner.

Town Meeting authorized the erection of the pound in 1797 and provided $20 for the purpose. It granted use of any stone found around the common with the exception of those needed for horse blocks and specified that the walls be five and one half feet high with a ten-inch timber of chestnut or white pine atop each one.

A field driver would bring stray animals to the pound and turn them over to the pound keeper who would hold them until their owners paid the necessary fine and endured a tongue-lashing. Anyone rash enough to attempt to rescue his stock without paying was fined 40 shillings. (Illustration by Helen Blackmer Flynn)

The '80s

RAGS and RICHES and TWO and ONE HALF

The decade of the '80s was a period of change for Sudbury, both in town government and on the street. New businesses popped up like mushrooms all along Route 20, many of them roundly criticized for their design and the increased traffic they caused.

Residents were torn between keeping the rural flavor of the community and caving in to the financial pressures of increased population and booming land values.

But the specter that hung over the community for nearly the entire decade was Proposition 2 1/2. Passed by a referendum in November of 1980, it sharply curtailed freewheeling spending in Sudbury, but also created a huge budget deficit of more than 11 percent in 1981.

Bill Downing retired after 30 years as town treasurer. When he started, the budget was $240,000. Now, in 1981, it was nearly $19 million.

Taxpayers experienced a case of sticker shock when their property was re-evaluated for the first time in ten years. Values had jumped from $191 million to $440 million in the last decade. Taxpayers formed a group called Citizens for Fair and Equal Revaluation to seek a review of revaluation work done by the independent assessing firm of McGee and Magane. Their claim that the new valuations didn't match up with sales prices didn't stand up and a meeting designed to confront town officials with the inequities fizzled.

A consultant hired by the town as a part of a long-range planning project advised that Sudbury, with its 6,300 acres of undeveloped land, should be going to condos, low- and medium-income housing, cluster zoning and apartments to save open space and increase tax dollars. The advice was largely ignored.

Despite a $1.50 reduction in the tax rate, the Selectmen report-
ed that the outlook for 1980 appeared bleak. They projected
deficits of $400,000, but noted the Town's cash position was
healthy at present and might balance out deficits for the current fiscal year. The Town approached Town Meeting with a
four-percent budget cap while inflation in most places was running in excess of 14 percent.

Ann Donald became Sudbury's first-ever woman Selectman,
John Anderson beat George Bush in the Republican primary
and the School Committee closed Fairbank School because of
declining enrollment.

The Town was festooned with yellow ribbons to celebrate the
return of the hostages from Iran in the winter of '81, but racial
problems cropped up between black and white students at
Lincoln-Sudbury Regional High School. This spawned the
school's first annual Human Relations Day with black comedi-
an and civil rights activist Dick Gregory attracting a crowd of
more than 1,000 and causing more controversy with some
inflammatory remarks.

Taxes went up for the second straight year and businessmen
were angered when they realized that their property was being
taxed 50 percent more than homeowners.

The assessment imbroglio made the headlines once more. "The
newly-installed property classification process is apparently
the cause of what may become the largest tax revolt in Sudbury
history since the Sudbury Suit of 1974," said former Selectman
John Powers.

The system, which specified that all property fall into one of
four categories: residential, commercial, industrial or open
space, drew the ire of Sudbury residents when the assessors,
together with assessing firm of McGee and Magane Inc., ruled
that no vacant land in Sudbury with the exception of plots that
fell into specific agricultural, forestry or farming categories,
could be rated as open space.

Instead, assessors decided that all vacant land be classified as
commercial land and be taxed at 150 percent of the residential

rate. The result, as Powers put it, "is a steadily increasing interest in what the possibilities (of escaping the ruling) are." Former town counsel David Turner cited the possibility of a class action suit addressing the problem of statutory interpretation.

Students Against Drunk Driving (SADD) formed a chapter at L-S; Fort Devens acquired 2,000 acres of land off Hudson Road for training purposes and warned residents of increased activity and noise in the area. The *Town Crier* reported a rash of "killer" dog attacks, resulting in the demise of four cats, one dog and nine chickens.

Back-to-back February snowstorms drained the town's snow removal budget in 1983 as controversy swirled around the proposed construction of a second building at the Star Market Plaza and an 82,000-square-foot shopping center, to be called Sudbury Crossing, on the site of Frank Vana's driving range on the Boston Post Road.

Route 20, its development and traffic, was on everyone's mind in 1984 and '85 with many residents going so far as expressing their concerns to the state Department of Public Works. In '86 hundreds of L-S students walked out in protest over staff reallocations brought about by school budget cuts. Dr. David Jackson was named Superintendent of the Elementary School System and soon had the School Committee singing his praises even though the Finance Committee found his ideas on education quite pricey.

In 1987 the Finance Committee faced the challenge of cutting $1.1 million from budget requests to stay under the levy limit of Proposition 2 1/2. The following year, amputee Diana Golden did the town proud by winning a gold medal in the 1988 Olympic Winter Games. She won the women's giant slalom for disabled skiers.

A July heat wave brought on a serious water crisis, and several teen suicides shook the community. Voters at Town Meeting approved a land transfer that led to the Longfellow Glen low-income housing project. The Housing authority submitted an article for 14 units of low-income family housing to shouts of

"Not In My Back Yard!" from neighbors. The *Town Crier* reported that Sudbury low-income housing developments could be approved through a comprehensive permit process by the state if snob zoning became an issue. Less than ten percent of the town's housing units qualified as low income.

Town Meeting nixed the low-income housing proposal as well as a land bank that would have been funded by a transfer tax. (An almost identical proposal was passed by Town Meeting in 1997).

The Housing Authority, under chairman Steven Swanger, continued to fight an uphill battle. It proposed senior housing for the Pierce rose farm property at the end of Maple Avenue (the former Frank Foss farm) only to have the initiative blocked. Swanger noted that there were no houses in Sudbury available for under $150,000 and the average new house was selling for $500,000, making it tough to bring in low-income housing, let alone buy it.

Swanger noted that 52 families were waiting for low-income housing with the average wait estimated at 10 to 15 years. He pointed out that needs were much greater in Sudbury than figures indicated. Most of the applicants were single-parent families with children. One couple lived in a tent in a parent's back yard until they could get help. The typical situation was a young mother with one or more kids living with her parents.

Open space took the spotlight in 1988. The town was divided over the construction of a bike trail to Lowell on the old New Haven railroad bed, 4.6 miles of which would run through the town.

Residents pushed the town for clearance of the "Desert," hundreds of acres of government land in West Sudbury which had become, according to the *Town Crier*: "a battlefield for Rambo-style war games, guns, rifles, stolen vehicles, refrigerators and stoves dumped and used for target practice, near other residential areas." Letters were addressed to the Sudbury, Hudson and Marlborough police departments. The request got fast results. By April, 100 abandoned cars were removed from Fort

Devens Annex, described by law enforcement officials as one of the biggest dumps in the state.

The Conservation Commission requested $6 million to acquire the Carding Mill pond area and 110 acres of land near the Wayside Inn. It was the largest amount of money ever requested for a piece of town land and was defeated at Town Meeting. Atkinson Pool opened at a cost of only $13,000 to the town with the Sudbury Foundation paying the other half.

Wayside Inn Historic District residents and landowners complained of a Planning Board article specifying five-acre lots for the land once owned by Henry Ford. The last of the deed restrictions imposed by Ford on the 1,210-acre area was due to run out by 1996. Town Meeting voted five-acre zoning for the entire Wayside Inn Historic district.

As 1988 wore on, two things were becoming clear: the Town's infrastructure was beginning to show signs of wear and tear and the student population of the Town was headed upward once again, some predictions said by 60 students a year. To make matters worse, the Dukakis Administration cut back sharply on state aid in order to balance its budget.

Another school would have to be re-opened, but which one? Nixon was more convenient and Loring had been sub-let to a group of vocal tenants, including a Synagogue, who wanted to stay put and argued that they were a benefit to the community. It was eventually decided that Nixon was a better choice.

The decision was made none too soon. Enrollment jumped by 80 students, prompting the School Committee to ask for a supplemental budget of $226,000. On the heels of this request, the Committee gave Superintendent of Schools David Jackson a whopping raise to more than $100,000. The Committee explained that it wanted to compensate Jackson on a level equal to other superintendents in the area since they considered him the best superintendent in the state. Jackson signed a three-year contract.

The Wayside Inn trustees found themselves the target of a barrage of faxes and letters from irate townspeople after they announced that popular innkeeper Frank Koppeis would step down in November of 1988. The trustees quickly reconsidered and allowed Koppeis to stay on the job until after the Town's 350th birthday celebration in 1989.

"All because of a misunderstanding," said Chairman Dan Coolidge, explaining that the rules of the Trust require that the innkeeper's pension fund no longer be funded after he reached age 70.

There were other important matters under constant discussion. Debate on a leash law for Sudbury's dogs stirred controversy. One letter to the *Town Crier* accused anti-leash-law advocates of not wanting to clean up after their animals.

Disposing of the Unisys (Sperry Rand) site on Route 117 ran into a snag because of water rules. Russ Kirby of the Planning Board cited a restriction on the use of the land and advised the Town to amend the zoning by-laws to address the problem.

Several fatal automobile accidents caused the Lincoln-Sudbury Regional School Committee to revise its open campus policy. Sophomores would no longer be able to leave the campus during school hours. Parents said they were seeking more structure and discipline. The open campus policy had been in effect since 1972.

The Goodnow Library celebrated its 125th Birthday with an open house and a speech by trustee and Town Historian Don Max. Earlier in the year the Goodnow family held its reunion in Sudbury and discovered that only one member of the family, Edgar Goodnow, a bachelor, still lived in town.

The Sudbury Historical Society announced that the Wood-Davison house, the oldest in Sudbury, would be moved to Sudbury Center for use as a headquarters and museum. The Society estimated the cost of moving the building to be $25,000 plus another $100,000 for basic restoration. The project was later abandoned.

A school study, completed late in 1988, predicted 2,500 students in Sudbury elementary schools by 1996 (the actual figure was 2,486). L-S was expected to drop to 850 by 1995.(It rose to 939).

Sudbury entered its 350th birthday year facing a crisis. School populations were rising, income from new construction that could be exempted from the Proposition 2 1/2 tax levy was shrinking and the Nixon and Noyes school buildings were beginning to fall apart. It was clear that the only way to accommodate all these needs was an override of Proposition 2 1/2, something that had never been accomplished successfully.

The Selectmen were preparing for the worst, coordinating an effort to complete a five-year financial plan by 1990. Its goal was to create clear financial guidelines which would be all-inclusive. The Board pointed out that a September 12th Special Town Meeting was called because of a $700,000-plus reduction in local aid from the State in fiscal year 1989.

"What will the '90s hold for us?" asked Chairman John Drobinski. "We suggest that it's the beginning of a 'reach for betterness.' We want the best for the Town Government of Sudbury, but it may require some minor reorganization or a complete Charter Commission. Sudbury has been a great town for the last 350 years, let's work on making it just a little bit better."

While all departments of the town scrambled to make cuts to reduce the budget shortfall, controversy boiled on another front. Unisys land developer Ralph Tyler, frustrated by the Town's inaction, demanded that the former Sperry Rand property be zoned for research and divided into three 25-acre parcels for better marketability. He indicated that he could claim compensation for restrictions and revert zoning regulations back to pre-1987 levels.

Meanwhile 350th Celebrations Chairman Beverly Bentley and her committee were putting the final touches to the Town's 350th birthday bash over the Labor Day weekend. The festivities, capped by the raising of the Mount Rushmore Flag, came off without a hitch. "Save the blueprints for the 400th!" trumpeted the *Town Crier*. It was a great party, for a great town.

XXIX

Tussling With Proposition 2 1/2

The news in the *1980 Sudbury Town Report* was both good and bad. The Selectmen proudly announced a $1.50 reduction in the tax rate, and, in the same breath, predicted a bleak financial year ahead. Sudbury's tax rate had risen only 2.2 percent in the last seven years, they pointed out, but what impact the tax-limiting referendum called "Proposition 2 1/2," scheduled to appear on the November general election ballot, would have on Sudbury's tax rate was anybody's guess.

Two and one half's premise seemed simple enough. It limited cities and towns to a two and one half percent increase in the tax levy over the previous year, forcing them to live within their means. But in a town like Sudbury with nearly 2,500 children enrolled in grades K through eight, it could mean Draconian cutbacks.

There were some in town who blamed the schools for the advent of 2 1/2. Since they were exempt from Town Meeting budget cutting, school administrators had become arrogant, and passing the Proposition seemed to be a good way to cut them down to size, even if it meant that other Town departments would have to take a hit as well.

The Selectmen projected deficits of $400,000, but noted that the Town's cash position was healthy and might balance out deficits for the coming fiscal year. They further cautioned that approaching Annual Town Meeting with a four percent tax cap when inflation was running at 14 percent was not healthy.

"Our main focus for next year is to maintain a stable tax rate," said Selectmen Chairman Robert Hotch. "But the job isn't going to be easy. We have been able to hold our house together financially so to speak but the state continues to make our job harder and harder.

"We were promised $5 million in new state local aid and only $166,000 was distributed. We were promised state takeover of County court costs and $13-$18 million is being assessed to cities and towns for courthouse rental fees. We were promised a certain amount on the cherry sheet...$55,000 short!" [1]

The first of many jolts came early. The Finance Committee was shocked by the near $1 million impact that the Lincoln Sudbury Regional High School assessment would have on Sudbury even though the school budget rose only by 3.9 percent. Part of the problem was an over-estimation of state aid for L-S. Even with a $243,000 cut mandated by the Finance Committee, school budgets were expected to impact the tax rate by $6 per thousand.

The cut was never made. The L-S School Committee voted a final budget of $5,879,901, an increase of 7.2 percent and nearly a million dollars over the previous year. Teachers lobbied for raises, saying there were no fat salaries. Committee member Alan Grathwohl noted that L-S had programs that were the envy of many small colleges. Four tenured teachers were dropped because of falling enrollment.

After a dip in state aid raised Sudbury taxes 58 cents a thousand and Fincom Chairman Joseph Slomski predicted that Special Town Meeting appropriations of $168,000 would raise the tax rate to $63.38, Executive Secretary Richard "Ed" Thompson organized a series of meetings between the Selectmen and other Town boards to set some priorities for the challenge ahead.

Early in this process, former Fincom chairman Ed Glazer was commissioned to prepare a report on the potential impact of Proposition 2 1/2. What he discovered wasn't encouraging. If there were no local override and no alternative sources of funding were forthcoming, the Town would have to reduce its spending by a whopping $1,570,000, a tad over 11 percent. Experts predicted that it would be impossible to cut the budget that severely without impacting town services. If the referendum passed, the 1981 Annual Town Meeting would be saddled with making the cuts.

"If 2 1/2 passes it will mean that towns such as Sudbury will have to depend more on state revenues to support local expenditures," said Glazer. "At Town meeting we will have a limit on the amount of property taxes that can be raised.

"Quite frankly, no one knows what the Massachusetts Legislature will do if 2 1/2 passes, either in terms of amending Proposition 2 1/2 or providing alternative sources of funding for local communities.

"As a former member of the Finance Committee, as a taxpayer of Sudbury and as a user of Town services, I am concerned about the potential impact of Proposition 2 1/2 on the Town's ability to continue to provide the kind and level of services that many of its citizens desire.

"I am equally concerned that passage of Proposition 2 1/2 will potentially interfere with the workings of Town Meeting and inhibit the town's ability to make intelligent decisions with respect to the financial issues facing Sudbury." [2]

After the referendum passed by a substantial margin, town departments met again to pinpoint possible cuts. A hypothetical budget prepared by the School Committee predicted that schools would be cut nearly a million dollars. Teachers advocated bussing cuts to save dollars and jobs.

The Selectmen detailed department cuts under 2 1/2: five police officers, no cruiser replacements, patrols drastically reduced, and four firefighters/EMTs laid off. The North Sudbury firehouse would be for housing of vehicles only. Ambulance replacement would be deferred. The schools might lose as many as 28 teachers.

"What about next year? Our most important job will be to take a leadership role in determining the allocation of scarce local resources," concluded Ann Donald, the town's first female selectman. "In making this determination, the town government, including all schools, must be considered as a whole unit which cannot remain healthy or viable if one of its parts is weakened or destroyed.

"Sudbury's town government runs very efficiently. We have amalgamated, centralized, studied cost benefits, made innovations...and we must continue to do more...but there is very little latitude after last year's 2 1/2 cuts to do much more budget cutting. We want to and we believe we can maintain current levels of services while giving appropriate cost-of-living salary increases. To do otherwise will have long-range effects that will be to the detriment of the town. It will be a difficult chore, but challenging, and we are dedicated to accomplishing the task."

The selectmen were as good as their word, and thanks to new construction money that was exempt from the Proposition 2 1/2 levy, the Town struggled through 1981 only to face another challenge early the following year. Thanks to a delay in the establishment of property valuation figures, the Town was unable to budget or appropriate funds up to the maximum allowed under Proposition 2 1/2. This meant the Town's tax levying capability for 1982 would be limited to one percent instead of two and one half percent. This translated into short-falls in fiscal 1984 and '85 of $350,000 and $600,000 respectively.

Again the Town was saved by the bell in the form of a windfall in state aid that allowed employees to receive a fair wage and goods and services to be delivered, but Sudbury wasn't out of the woods yet. The reduced tax levy left Sudbury $300,000 under its maximum assessment. If this was not corrected, the Finance Committee warned, it would undermine the Town's ability to raise needed funds in future years.

For the second year in a row a windfall of $408,000 in local state aid and a one-time $185,800 MBTA abatement saved the day, but presented a problem as well. If the excess monies were used to cut real estate taxes, the Town's tax-levying capability under Proposition 2 1/2 would again be reduced.

So the Town found itself in the strange position of calling a Special Town Meeting in October to find a way to keep from reducing taxes.

The dilemma was this: if the Town used the increased state aid to lower taxes, the total tax levy--the amount collected in taxes-

-would also fall below the $12.2 million dollar limit allowed by Proposition 2 1/2. The following year, under the requirements of Proposition 2 1/2 the Town could increase its levy by no more than 2.5 percent of this year's levy.

"Any significant reduction below this year's limit would automatically reduce the levy limits in future years," explained Finance Committee Chairman James Pitt. "If the levy limit is thus reduced, and unless free cash is available, jobs and services will have to be eliminated to balance the budget."

Pitt pointed out that several options were available: 1. The funds could be used for requests facing Town Meeting. 2. Establishment of a stabilization fund or reduce the amount of free cash to be applied to town expenditures. He noted that the stabilization fund article on the warrant would allow Town Meeting the option of putting aside extra revenue to be reappropriated in later years when the Town's financial situation might not be as sound.

The voters at Town Meeting chose a combination of the two, approving plans to demolish or renovate Fairbank School, renovations of the town offices and the resurfacing of several roads as well as establishing a stabilization fund "bank" to deal with unanticipated local state aid and MBTA abatements. The appropriation of $293,654 from the Town's free cash account to offset the tax rate, already approved by the Annual Town Meeting, was allowed to stand.

Again, the solution was a temporary one. By May of 1983, Thompson told the Selectmen that the Town was already $3.9 million in the hole and would most likely have to borrow again. The Town was already paying $50 a day in interest. Two months later, that situation changed when the Town learned it would receive more State aid for fiscal year 1984 than expected. Once again the Finance Committee had to figure out a way to cook the books or face lower potential for tax revenue in coming years.

When all the numbers were added up, the Town's previously determined tax levy was found to be $443,438 under what it was entitled to under Proposition 2 1/2. If the levy was not brought up to the limit this year, it would be further restricted in future years.

Thompson calculated that $466,123 would be needed in free cash to cover the Town's expenses. Cherry Sheet figures revealed that Sudbury would be receiving $414,484 more than had been estimated and that the free cash commitment was now too high. The new money pushed the tax levy down to $12,286,254 or $443,438 below the 2 1/2 levy limit.

A Special Town Meeting in October quickly solved the problem, appropriating monies for repairs, town services, unpaid bills and debt service as well as tax relief for the blind and elderly.

"The state of the town is excellent!" reported the Selectmen in 1985. "The level of funding voted at the April Town Meeting and October Special Town Meeting will maintain essential services without creating any real hardships. Two major reasons we've been able to live within Prop 2 1/2 are: 1. Prudent use of free cash and 2. New construction ($8 million of commercial and $23 million of residential). The Town is able to maintain the posture we have in both schools and town government because of wise use of Town funds and planning ahead."

New construction and rising property values kept the Town humming in 1985 and '86 despite fears of the elimination of federal revenue sharing programs which were worth #130,000 to Sudbury in fiscal year 1986. Property values had risen 30 percent from the previous evaluation in 1976. Houses now averaged over $175,000 and land $75,000 an acre. The tax rate, currently $22.06 for residents and $36.55 for commercial and businesses, was expected to drop significantly.

The euphoria continued well into 1988. "Other cities and towns would be envious of our financial position," chortled the Selectmen. "A good feeling was running rampant in our community... one of togetherness. Much was accomplished with citizen involvement as it should be, and the town government contributed its resources as requested...hopefully we can keep up the momentum."

Money was coming in from all directions. Taxes on new construction that took place in 1985 added $590,000 to the amount the town could spend in 1986. Cherry Sheet aid and an insurance rebate yielded a $150,000 windfall in '86, allowing the Finance Committee to restore $143,000 to department budgets. Late in 1987 the Assessors announced that $39,865,694 had been added to the tax base through real estate and personal property tax valuations.

But early in 1988 there were signs that the good times were ending. Construction--especially commercial construction--was tapering off and the Town's birth rate had increased 50 percent since 1977. The handwriting was on the wall; more classroom space was needed in a hurry. There was only one problem: No state reimbursement money for new school construction would be available in the near future. If the Town wanted a new school, it was on its own.

Superintendent of Schools Dr. David Jackson had more in mind than just a new school. He shocked the Finance Committee early in 1988 with a 16.8 percent increase in the school budget. Sixty percent of the hike would cover increased enrollment and the other 40 percent was for enhancement. Jackson planned to hire six new teachers for enrollment and 4.2 more teachers to implement planned new programs.

Jackson fretted that Curtis Middle School had one teacher per 23.9 students while Wayland and Weston had 20 pupils per teacher. Of 19 communities surveyed, he pointed out, Sudbury paid less per pupil than 12. Sudbury's cost per pupil was $3,801 as against $5,441 for Lincoln, the most expensive. Jackson also asked for $500,000 for maintenance projects, which had been delayed for several years.

The Finance Committee noted that if all School Committee requests were met, police officers would have to be pulled off the street, and Chairman David Wilson warned that the 1989 budget was headed for an override vote unless $1.8 million was cut.

But something had to be done. Enrollment projections showed that between 70 and 100 new students a year would be entering the system for the next six years, reflecting a 50 percent increase in Sudbury's birth rate since 1977. The School Committee proposed an $11 million program to create three K-5 elementary schools using the Haynes, Noyes and Nixon buildings and adding from 24,400 to 37,500 square feet of new classroom space.

Architectural services to design the new additions and renovations were projected at $750,000, a sum that would increase the tax levy beyond the limits of Proposition 2 1/2. It appeared that the Town's will would be tested by referendum for the first time.

As it turned out, three referendum questions were considered but never faced voters in 1988. A $1 million senior center behind Goodnow Library, $750,000 in architect's fees for the new school proposal, and $40,000 for renovations at L-S, which had already been approved by Town Meeting and completed. Fincom Chairman Wilson explained that exempting that $40,000 from 2 1/2 would free up a like amount which could be used in the Town's operating budget the following year.

The $750,000 in architects fees for the renovations and additions to Nixon School were finally approved by a Special Town Meeting, April 4, 1988, and the town appropriated $15,000 to plan the expansion of Fairbank School into a Senior Center.

Meanwhile the School Committee laid plans to look for an extra $323,000 on the Town Meeting floor, either from another department or a Proposition 2 1/2 override. The Finance Committee had recommended a K-8 budget of $6,789,446, in itself a 13.6 percent raise over the previous year. The Committee's efforts were unsuccessful. Town Meeting approved an $8,367,086 budget which included debt.

The rumblings of upcoming disaster in 1989 continued through the summer. Superintendent of Schools Jackson sought a preliminary 8 1/2 to 13 percent increase in the school budget which eventually ballooned to a 22 percent increase or $10,199,820.

Something was going to happen, but no one in Sudbury had any idea just what.

XXX

Override!

As Sudbury's 350th birthday year began, the talk on the street, in the shops and at the town offices was of money. The Selectmen began coordinating an effort to complete a five-year financial plan to be ready early in 1990. Its goal was to create clear, all-inclusive financial guidelines. Goals for the '90s would include a new fire headquarters, a resource recovery program at the dump, relocation of the Wood-Davison house from the Post Road to Sudbury Center, and enterprise funds that would eventually make the dump and Atkinson Pool self-sufficient.

It was obvious that the school system faced a budget squeeze unlike any that it had ever faced before. The Fincom directed the L-S School Committee to prepare a six-percent increase budget and a level-funded budget. Committee Chairman Dick Brooks responded that jobs would be cut and questioned how the school was going to function.

The schools weren't the only ones getting the word. Fire Chief Michael Dunne and Police Chief Peter Lembo were both told that without a general override of Proposition 2 1/2, jobs would have to be cut. Librarian Bill Talentino noted that his facility would lose $26,000 if the override failed, forcing him to cut library hours drastically.

Superintendent David Jackson pointed out that no override would mean fewer teachers and larger class sizes. He foresaw many parents sending their children to private schools. He noted that he had already laid off certain middle-administrators because of 2 1/2 in 1983 and hadn't hired them back. There wasn't that much fat to cut.

Jackson also noted that he had to add $465,000 for expansion and interim space to handle an increased enrollment and had already cut that figure to $320,000 in his 16-percent increase budget. He further noted that the average elementary school teacher in Sudbury was making $39,000 annually. Starting teachers received $21,000 and those with Masters degrees and 16 years in the system earned $42,000.

By early February, things had gotten very serious. The Selectmen decided to put the override questions on the general town election ballot, but expressed concern on the impact of a "no override" vote. Executive Secretary Ed Thompson contacted the Massachusetts Department of Revenue to see what options the town had if the override should fail.

The stakes and the numbers were high. The Fincom pondered going for a $2.5 million override or possibly a $1 million request, pending a hearing to be held February 15 at the Town Hall. "If the override fails, every single department goes down the tubes. Either everybody makes it or no one does," said Chairman Jack Hepting.

The final override number was $1,896,680 after the School Committee submitted a 16 percent budget increase but withdrew its proposed $8.5 million construction project at Nixon School.

Now the selling began. The Selectmen explained that Sudbury's growth was slowing down. The Town had benefitted in the last five years from new revenue brought in by new property purchasers, $1.86 million in fiscal 1990 and $2.83 million in fiscal 1989, which was no longer there. Income from new construction was significantly lower than the previous four years.

Former Fincom Chairman Marjorie Wallace, writing in opposition to the override in the *Town Crier*, noted that 60 percent of the town's residents couldn't afford it and suggested that it was time for the town to bring its spending back under control. She pointed out that the Town had increased its spending 26 percent over the past three fiscal years. Nine of the 22 teaching positions to be cut at Lincoln-Sudbury would be eliminated anyway because of decreasing enrollment, she said.

More than 150 people jammed lower Town Hall on February 15 for an open discussion of the pros and cons of an override, something that The Town had never done successfully before. Opponents worried aloud that people would lose control and overrides would go on year after year. Proponents supported the override because they wanted quality education and were afraid property values would drop should education quality decline.

As the election approached, a half-page ad paid for by *Citizens to Preserve Fiscal Responsibility Within Town Government*, appeared in the *Town Crier*. It urged defeat of the override. "If the override wins, your taxes will go up 20 percent. Do you really think our quality of life will collapse if we vote no?" it reasoned.

Lincoln-Sudbury was also putting on the full court press. L-S School Committee member Harry Nogelo declared that the L-S budget had to increase 6.9 percent just to deal with state-mandated costs. Students whined about saving their teachers. Ed McCarthy of the Sudbury Teachers Assn. urged parents to vote the override and keep good teachers in place. Separate feelings on taxes and education, the Association said while turning the screws a little tighter by publishing a list of those to be fired if the override wasn't successful.

On March 27, 1989, the voters spoke. The $1.8M override proposal was defeated 2831-1705 while a proposal for the construction of a Senior center passed by 10 percent. "The Town is going to have to tighten its belt" said Thompson. "I think the voters are unhappy about something and they definitely don't want an override in the magnitude of $1.89 million."

"I do almost see it as a mandate to town officials to take a look at how things are run," said Wallace. "I think it was an educated decision," added Selectman John Drobinski. "I'm disappointed with the vote, but the townspeople have spoken."

Town Meeting got the message, quickly passing a level-funded budget that would fit under the 2 1/2 cap. The School Committee announced that it would work within its budget and not ask for additional funding.

"Clearly the message has been sent to the schools that we can't have the money the School Committee wanted," said Chairman Steven Bober. "This isn't a question of belt tightening. The belt is around our necks. I think the town has to understand what's going to happen."

Some of the moves were immediate. Parents howled when the School Committee voted to study discontinuing bussing within a mile of schools if walkways were available, but Selectman David Wallace urged the town to pull together and not single out individual groups for criticism. Barely three weeks following the meeting, interim Lincoln-Sudbury Superintendent-Principal Robert Gardner announced plans to release 15 teachers and added he was studying a plan to institute athletic user fees in order to trim his budget by $582,000, the limit allowed by the 2 1/2 tax cap.

But the wolves were already at the door. In the November 9, 1989 edition of the *Town Crier* was a quarter page ad taken out by the Cambridge School of Weston. "A good education doesn't depend on surprises," it said.

XXXI

Finding Space and Money

While the controversy over Proposition 2 1/2 had been settled, the School Committee still had a big problem. Since the end of the 1989 school year, 60 school-age kids had moved into town and only 25 had moved out. More school space was needed and needed in a hurry. To make matters worse, Cherry Sheet cuts brought on by the Dukakis Administration budget deficit resulted in a Town budget shortfall of some $775,000, a reduction of more than 17 percent, only part of which would be covered by an eight percent increase in the tax rate.

The School Committee was taking a hard line. It prepared two budgets for FY 91, one with override and one without and brazenly called for the renovation and expansion of the Nixon school for $9.95 million. "It's time to make an issue of what we believe," the Committee announced. "Let's renovate Nixon for quality space for a quality program that we believe children deserve." Shortly before a Special Town Meeting, the committee hedged its bet by including an alternate proposal that would renovate Nixon for $4.15 million and put off expansion until a later date.

Meanwhile the Town Fathers were hoping the assessors would bail them out by discovering unalloted funds in the abatement accounts. These overlay accounts are set aside yearly in case of abatements or refunds. The Assessors came up with $353,167.05 and were immediately asked by the Selectmen to come up with $150,000 more. A total of $775,000 was needed to balance the budget.

The Fincom responded by proposing a "menu" of override selections. Jack Hepting's five-year financial planning ad hoc committee estimated a $675,000 shortfall for fiscal year 1991, meaning either service cuts or a 2 1/2 override. The menu gave voters the choice of an escalating series of cuts, each accompanied by a series of additional services it would allow.

On October 19, Special Town Meeting approved a modified $3.651 million proposal that would renovate Nixon school. A month and a day later, a debt exemption override for the project was passed 1,327--1,217, a margin of 110 votes.

Down the road at Lincoln-Sudbury, new Superintendent Matt King was having his problems. The combination of the previous April's override failure and a declining enrollment was making even the most basic of services harder to deliver. Sports budgets were cut in half, prompting the Lincoln-Sudbury Boosters Club to organize a door-to-door fund drive, which raised $27,500.

King told the School Committee that a preliminary estimate of the cost of the current programs at L-S would require $9.172 million, some $772,000 more than what was expected to be available in FY 1991. The choices available to him were both Draconian--either larger class sizes or fewer course offerings.

Parents on both the high school and elementary levels were in a quandary. Many supported overriding Proposition 2 1/2 in order to give their children a better education and keep property values high, but they were outvoted by older residents seeking to keep taxes within reason during a time when a shortfall of state aid put a heavier burden on local taxpayers.

Many feared that budget cuts would hurt the competitiveness of public schools and some--around 15 percent--opted for private school educations.

As Sudbury's seventh half-century came to a close, another blow landed. A second reduction in state aid left the town with a million dollar shortfall. But this time, nobody panicked. The Town had gone through so much during the past decade that a million dollars didn't seem like such a big deal. If everybody pulled together, the money could be found someplace.

And so it was. Just as they had for 350 years, the residents of Sudbury closed ranks to face a common foe. This time the opposition wasn't King Philip's warriors or the soldiers of Britain's General Gage, but a simple budget shortfall. It all boiled down to one simple premise: give everybody a fair shake.

XXXII

A Year of Coming Together

Sunday, September 3, 1989 dawned a bluebird day in Sudbury and Beverly Bentley breathed a sigh of relief. One down, two to go. If the weather would hold for only another 48 hours, Sudbury's 350th anniversary would be over and, hopefully, a success.

Bentley was understandably nervous. Three years of planning and fund raising had gone into this birthday bash and she and her committee were determined to produce something special.

The events had started the previous spring with two sellout performances of "Town Meeting Tonight," an original musical written by Dr. Bill Adelson and produced by Virginia Kirschner. The Harvard-Radcliffe Orchestra joined the combined Sudbury church choirs for a sold-out concert in April; the Sudbury Minute and Militia held a Colonial Heritage Weekend in May and a delegation of Sudbury residents led by retired Selectman Ann Donald visited Sudbury, Suffolk, in England's East Anglia region to extend an invitation to Mayor Sylvia Byham to join the festivities. In August, four busloads of citizens attended Sudbury night at Fenway Park.

A 350th logo design contest was held and Meredith Palmer's winning entry was soon on caps, T-shirts and sweatshirts being worn by nearly everyone in town. The clothing sale raised more than $15,000 which was eventually returned to the Town. Thanks to adroit fund raising and contributions from local merchants, the year-long celebration didn't cost the Town a cent aside from police overtime.

In early August, the Committee revealed its celebration weekend plans to the Town. The parade would start at Lincoln-Sudbury Regional High School and end at Raytheon. Bands scheduled to march included the U.S.S. Constitution honor guard, Ancient and Honorable Artillery Co. of Massachusetts, Fort Devens Band, Needham Military Band, the Blue Knights

Motorcycle Club, Sudbury Companies of Militia and Minute, and Sudbury Ancient Fife and Drum Corps.

There would be more than ten different neighborhood floats plus various civic groups and organizations, all competing for $800 in prizes. (The committee underestimated here. Fifty-two separate units marched in the parade including 28 floats and five bands.) President Bush and Senators Ted Kennedy and John Kerry and Governor Michael Dukakis had been invited. Special 350th first-day-of-issue cachets for stamp collectors would be available at Bentley's Stationers and a Post Office van would be parked at the Sudbury Inn Marketplace to cancel them on September 4, the 350th anniversary of Sudbury's incorporation.

The first evening of the celebration went off without a hitch, Ruth Brown cut the Official Town birthday cake, donated by Marrone's Bakery, and everyone had a slice before enjoying a night of dancing. Five bands, featuring everything from the big band sound of the Suburbanaires to Rock and Roll and Dixieland jazz played at various halls around the common, the sound of their music wafting through the twilight as townspeople strolled the blocked-off streets and stopped to chat with friends and neighbors.

Sunday's activities were to center around the Lincoln-Sudbury athletic fields where a field day, picnic and flag raising would be climaxed by a laser light show after dark. Dozens of tents and marquees had been set up along the edges of the fields where they offered every sort of craft and ethnic food imaginable. Kids participated in competitions and games, got their faces painted by itinerant artists, went for a hayride, or listened to story tellers while their parents tried their hands at horseshoe pitching and other games.

During the morning, volunteers had cordoned off a large area of the Lincoln-Sudbury High School's north parking area where a large crane donated by Joseph Piazzi and the New England Crane Company, and several cannons of the Massachusetts Tenth Artillery Battery were waiting to receive the Mount Rushmore Flag.

Commissioned in 1986 by the National Park Service, the 45 by 90 foot, 330-pound flag is an official exhibit of the Department of the Interior Take Pride in America Program. Its stars and stripes were made in different parts of the country and were assembled at the John F. Kennedy Library. It flies only at official functions of state, with the President, or at very, very special ceremonies.

As more than 8,000 townspeople gathered around, the flag was removed from its solid cherry chest by volunteers and secured to a 1.5-ton spar attached to the crane. The wood for the chest was gathered in each of the 13 towns of Plymouth County commemorating the original 13 colonies. The chest and flag are based at the Boston Historic Park at the Charlestown Navy Yard aboard the U.S.S. Constitution.

The 10th Battery's cannon boomed out a 21-gun salute and the strains of the National Anthem filled the air as the crane slowly raised the spar. Each volunteer clung to the edge of the flag until the very last minute before being forced to let go, and then stood in place and saluted until the flag cleared the ground and waved in the gentle breeze. There wasn't a dry eye within earshot.

"The Mt. Rushmore flag pulled everybody together," Bentley recalled later. "During the raising of the flag I just happened to look back around me and here was a gentleman standing near me. I didn't know who he was but he was standing there giving the traditional salute with the tears just streaming down his face. What memories that must have brought back to him."

The National Park Service had contacted Bentley's Committee and offered to fly the Mount Rushmore Flag at the field day provided the Town would arrange and pay for the crane and the operator. "On a Friday night late I was literally looking through the phone book for a crane company," Bentley recalled. "I called this company in Framingham and this fellow answered the phone said 'Yes, I can do that but you'll have to pay the driver because it's a holiday.' I went to Raytheon and they picked up the $2,000 tab for the driver and National Park Service expenses. We really lucked out. It didn't cost the town a penny."

As the sun set that evening, music from the Cantabridgia Brass Quartet drifted across the field and finally it was really dark. The thousands seated around the field and on the hill near Concord Road saw the lights go out all around them and watched the first beams of the laser show march across the school wall. They watched as townspeople, not activists. The Mount Rushmore flag had drawn them together as one.

"Family Day at the High School Grounds brought out citizens of all ages," wrote Mary Jane Hillery in the *Town Crier*. "Everyone was part of the community family as well. The common bond of being part of the Sudbury celebration made everyone brothers and sisters for the day. The only credential you needed was the joy of being part of a birthday celebration worth waiting 350 years for."

"The biggest highlight was the way the people and committees worked together to get it done," said Bentley. "We had the plans, but it would have never come off if people like Hal Cutler and Lois Toeppner and others hadn't pitched in. Even to this day it impresses me. Harold set up that whole transportation system and Lois was in charge of the Saturday night dances.

"The night of the dance I was talking to [Chief of Police] Pete Lembo. He was sitting there having one of his cigars and he said: 'I can't believe it. We have so many people wandering around this town and there are absolutely no problems.' We had no problems, no arrests for the whole weekend. There was no disorderly conduct. Everybody was wonderful."

There was still the grand parade on Labor Day with retiring Wayside Inn Innkeeper Frank Koppeis as Grand Marshal and Mayor Sylvia Byham of Sudbury, Suffolk, England and her husband Roy, and Mayor Peter Wong and his wife Lynn of Sudbury, Ontario, as special guests, but it was almost an anticlimax. While the floats and clowns and fire engines were fun, people came away remembering where they were and what they did when the Mount Rushmore flag was raised skyward.

Forgotten was the rancor from the previous spring's battles over the Proposition 2 1/2 override which had failed. On this day, people weren't pro-education or anti-affordable housing;

they were just neighbors and friends who happened to live in a town called Sudbury. The financial battles would go on into the next decade and beyond, but there would always be consensus and the Town would go on as before.

Perhaps Selectman John Drobinski put it best in the *1989 Town Report*. "The aftermath of the celebration left a common thought in our minds," he wrote. "It was a year of coming together."

Endnotes

Chapter I

1. *Sudbury Enterprise*, September 7, 1889
2. *Lowell Weekly Journal*, April, 1887
3. Katherine Bradshaw Interview by the author
4. *Annals of the Town of Sudbury*, p. 31, p. 40

Chapter II

1. Proceedings at the Dedication of the Soldiers and Sailors Monument at Sudbury, Massachusetts, June 17th, 1896, remarks of Jonas S. Hunt, p. 31

Chapter III

1. *1889 Sudbury Town Report*
2. *1890 Sudbury Town Report*
3. *1891 Sudbury Town Report*
4. *1892 Sudbury Town Report*
5. *1897 Sudbury Town Report*
6. *1898 Sudbury Town Report*
7. Superintendent Curlew's report, 1900 *Sudbury Town Report*
8. *1901 Sudbury Town Report*
9. *1911 Sudbury Town Report*

10. *1919 Sudbury Town Report*
11. *Lowell Weekly Journal*, 1892, n.d.
12. *Lowell Weekly Journal*, September, 1897

Chapter IV

1. The material for this chapter was taken from a reminiscence
   written by Atherton Rogers in 1917 now in the
   Bradshaw-Rogers collection at the Wayside Inn
   Archives.

Chapter VI

1. Wayside Inn Hostess Diary, October 28, 1942
2. Oral history tape of Alvin Noyes, Lincoln-Sudbury Regional
   High School Library
3. *The Life that Ruth Built*, New York Times Book Company,
   1975

Chapter VII

1. Wayside Inn Archives, Solicitation for Support of Wayside
   Inn Trust
2. *Boston Herald*, June 1956 Article by Frank Noyes. Story was
   told to him by Charles Hovey Pepper who heard it from
   Brooks himself
3. Boston News Bureau, July 13, 1924
4. Wayside Inn Archives
5. 1939 *Sudbury Town Report*, pp. 6-7

Chapter VIII

1. Clarence Ames Interview, 1996
2. *Framingham News*, August 11, 1925
3. Sudbury Town Archives
4. *Framingham News*, August 20, 1925

Chapter IX

1. Clips from *Boston Globe, Boston Transcript,* and other media regarding the Cape Cod and Sudbury Propriety litigation assembled in a scrapbook by Forrest Bradshaw. Bradshaw-Rogers Collection, Sudbury Historical Society archives
2. *The Rebirth and Death of the Propriety of Sudbury Plantation,* Richard W. Francis thesis. Copy in Sudbury Historical Society archives
3. Bradshaw-Rogers Collection, Sudbury Historical Society archives
4. 1929 *Sudbury Town Report* pp. 42-43

Chapter X

1. Mildred Tallant interview, 1997
2. *1931 Sudbury Town Report*
3. *Ibid*

Chapter XII

1. Wayside Inn Hostess Diaries, 1938
2. Leona Johnson interview, 1996
3. Mildred Tallant interview, 1997
4. Natalie Eaton interview, 1996
5. Wayside Inn Hostess Diaries, 1938
6. *Ibid*
7. Goodnow Library scrapbook collection

Chapter XIII

1. *Boston Globe,* July 3, 1939
2. *Sudbury Beacon,* July 7, 1939

Chapter XIV

1. *Sudbury Beacon,* February 23, 1940
2. Eyewitness statements re: Kalilianen Case, C.F. Garfield private collection
3. Sudbury Selectmen's minutes, December 11, 1941

4. *Framingham News*, December 30, 1941

Chapter XV

1. *American Legion Newsletter*, May 1944
2. *1944 Sudbury Town Report*, pp. 6-15
3. *American Legion Newsletter*, September, 1944
4. *Ibid*
5. *American Legion Newsletter*, January, 1945
6. *American Legion Newsletter* No. 12
7. *American Legion Newsletter* No. 15

Chapter XVI

1. Wayside Inn Hostess Diaries, January 19, 1946
2. Wayside Inn Archives

Chapter XVII

Chapter XVIII

1. *Town Crier*, December 17, 1981
2. *1955 Sudbury Town Report*, pp. 10-11
3. *Ibid*
4. *Ibid* pp. 104-112
5. *Ibid* pp. 212-220
6. *Sudbury Citizen*, February 8, 1958

Chapter XIX

This chapter was written from newspaper accounts (available at the Wayside Inn Archives) as well as personal interviews with many of the participants.

Chapter XX

1. *Sudbury Citizen*, January 22, 1959
2. *Ibid*, February 11, 1959
3. *Ibid*, February 18, 1959

4. Sudbury Water District Report, 1959, Sudbury Town
     Archives
5. *Sudbury Citizen*, May 7, 1959

Chapter XXII

1. *Sudbury 1959 Town Report*, p. 164
2. *Sudbury Citizen*, May 14, 1959
3. *Sudbury 1959 Town Report*, p. 82
4. *Sudbury Citizen*, November 25, 1959
5. *Ibid*, December 3, 1959
6. *Sudbury 1959 Town Report*, p. 13

Chapter XXIII

1. *Sudbury Citizen*, March 3, 1966
2. *Sudbury 1966 Town Report*

Chapter XXIV

1. *Sudbury Fence Viewer*, November 27, 1963
2. *We shall Not Tamely Give It Up* by John C. Powers.
     Privately Published. Available at Goodnow Library

Chapter XXV
The '70s

1. *Sudbury Citizen*, August 30, 1973
2. *Ibid*, September 26, 1973

Chapter XXVI

This chapter was written by Anthony Moore, ex-Mayor and Town Councillor of Sudbury, Suffolk, England, as a report to his Town Council following his participation in Sudbury's Bicentennial activities in 1976.

Chapter XXVII

1. *Sudbury Citizen*, May 30, 1974
2. *Ibid*, June 25, 1975
3. *Ibid*, October 14, 1975
4. *1976 Sudbury Town Report*, pp. 10-14
5. *Sudbury Town Crier*, August 7, 1975
6. *Ibid*, November 26, 1975
7. *Ibid*, December 18, 1975

Chapter XXVIII

1. *Sudbury Citizen*, March 7, 1974
2. *Ibid*, July 25, 1974
3. *Ibid*, August 1, 1974

Chapter XXIX

1. *1980 Sudbury Town Report*
2. Report: *Potential Impact of Proposition 2 1/2* by Edward Glazer. Sudbury Town Archives
3. *1980 Sudbury Town Report*

Chapter XXXI

1. *Town Crier*, August 3, 1989
2. *Ibid*, October 5, 1989
3. *Ibid*, November 2, 1989

INDEX